Suicide &
Psychological
Pain

Prevention That Works

Published by
PESI Publishing & Media
PESI, Inc
3839 White Ave
Eau Claire, WI 54703

Cover Design: Amy Rubenzer

Library of Congress Cataloging-in-Publication Data

Klott, Jack.

Suicide and psychological pain : prevention that works / by Jack Klott.

p. cm.

ISBN 978-1-936128-16-7 (pbk.)

1. Suicide. 2. Suicide--Prevention. I. Title.

HV6545.K534 2012

616.85'8445--dc23

2012008793

PESI
Publishing
& Media
www.pesipublishing.com

Dedication

For my mentors: Beth McShane, MSW; Keith Eldridge, MSW; Josephus Hicks, MSW; Phyllis Hemmer, MSW; and, most importantly, Rebecca Klott, Ph.D.

Contents

Introduction

Before I begin this exploration of suicidal and self-harming clients and their behaviors, I believe it is important to emphasize some of the issues that are involved in understanding and working with this special population. As I reflect on my career of over 40 years as a provider of mental health services, I want to acknowledge the contributions of the pioneers of this field. Certainly no work on suicide or self-harm behaviors is complete without respecting the essential contribution of Edwin Shneidman, the founder of the American Association of Suicidology. Dr. Shneidman will be quoted extensively throughout this book due, in no small measure, to my respect for this gentleman. He is the one person whose insights into self-harm behaviors have given us the opportunity to understand, and sometimes to prevent, this ultimate tragedy.

Others who will be acknowledged for their contributions will include Harry Stack Sullivan, Joseph Sabbath, Ronald Maris, Jerome Motto, David Clark, Robert Litman, John Maltsberger, Aaron Beck, Marsha Linehan, Alan Berman, David Lester, John McIntosh, Bruce Bongar, Robert Yufit, David Brent, and William Miller. But, most important, I acknowledge those men and women who over the last four decades have given me the privilege of "getting to know them" and cautiously encouraged me to undertake a journey with them into the realm of their pain. Indeed, I will stress to the reader that the basis of understanding suicide and self-harm behaviors is in understanding the person experiencing these traumas. It is the stated goal of this book for the reader to gain a respect for *The Person* who is experiencing a suicidal episode and not merely the behavior. Harry Stack Sullivan reminded us in 1954 (p. 52) to approach our clients with the question "who is this person, and how does he/she come to be here?"

We treat people—NOT behaviors. I am sure that most readers are sensitive to the difference. Unfortunately, it is all too easy to lose track of this in working with the suicidal population. We become engrossed in "lethality assessments," "risk assessments," "safety plans" and other such vehicles that place entirely too much emphasis on the behavior and miss the point of WHY this person is experiencing a suicidal crisis in the first place. Shneidman (1954) wrote, "the first task of therapy is to discover the locus of the client's unbearable pain and to decrease the perturbation associated with that condition." Asking our client, "where do you hurt?" will often reveal to us the focus of the suicidal intent or the purpose of the self-harm behaviors. People do what they do for a reason; all behaviors are purposeful. This is essential in understanding suicide and self-harm behaviors. It is a purpose-driven behavior designed either to eliminate or manage unbearable levels of pain in their current life circumstances. Our clients therefore view these behaviors as beneficial, attractive, and helpful. Our clinical view of suicide and self-harm behaviors is, typically, to pathologize them. We view suicide as dysfunctional, maladaptive. Our clients, however, have a different perspective. We must develop an empathic view of our clients' approach to suicide and recognize it is their method of managing pain. It is our endeavor, therefore, in the context of a caring relationship, to assist our client in the discovery of the sources of their pain and to provide them with alternatives—as Shneidman said "removing their blinders"—for solving and managing these issues in their lives.

This book will explore that struggle. We examine the nature of this perturbation—what Shneidman (1985) calls "psychache"—and how we can assist our client in the discovery of "alternative ways to manage life's traumas." It's all about providing them with options—alternatives to suicide.

One final word on this approach: Because of the important consideration that our clients' view of suicide and self-harm behaviors are beneficial and attractive coping strategies, we are reminded that they are not going to be inclined to accept our offer of "alternative strategies for reducing their pain" without motivation. Therefore, the role of *Motivation* is vital in helping our clients change their behaviors In their book, *Motivational Interviewing*, Miller and Rollnick (1992), urge us to remember that "nobody changes behaviors without motivation." Therefore, throughout this book we are going to remind the reader about the vital role of why and how this "motivation" is essential in inviting our clients to accept our offer of learning alternative ways of managing their pain.

Let us begin our discussion of suicide and self-harm behaviors. As noted, this book is reliant on the valuable works of the men and women noted above and also, perhaps more to the point, on the lessons I have learned from my clients – young and old — who, at a painful time in their lives, viewed suicide and self-harm as their "only" recourse in assuaging their unbearable pain or solving seemingly intractable problems.

Where does our information on suicide come from? The information gathered for this book comes from my clients, but also from clinical studies on suicide. And herein lays the challenge regarding the study of suicide. When medical science goes about learning the varied aspects of medical disorders they will, normally, have a live subject in their clinic being interviewed and examined which will result in valuable information regarding the conditions and factors inherent in various medical conditions. Such is not the case in studies of completed suicide where the subjects we need to talk to are not available due to their tragic deaths. Hence, the development of the *psychological autopsy*. It is through this method that examiners reconstruct the completed suicide victim's life through interviews with their loved ones. The essential ingredients of the psychological autopsy method include face-to-face interviews with knowledgeable informants within months of the death.

David Clark in *The Assessment and Prediction of Suicide* (1992, p. 144) defines this process: "the 'psychological autopsy' refers to a procedure for reconstructing an individual's psychological life after the fact (of their suicide), particularly the person's lifestyle and those thoughts, feelings, and behaviors manifested during the weeks and months preceding death, in order to achieve a better understanding of the psychological, behavioral, and psychiatric circumstances contributing to a death." Why are these psychological autopsies necessary? Not long ago information on suicide was gathered from interviews with people who had made non-fatal suicide attempts and/or with men and women in clinical treatment who had discussed suicide with a therapist. It became clear in various studies (Linehan, 1986) that neither of these populations truly represented people who die by suicide. As a matter of fact, studies by Stengel and Cook (1958) revealed that people whose suicide activities are limited to suicidal ideation and non-fatal attempts and people who die by suicide "are more different than alike." As another example, Rich, Young, and Fowler (1986) noted that over half of those who die by suicide have "never received any mental health treatment in their lifetimes."

The phrase "psychological autopsy" was initially used by Shneidman in his early work in 1951. He, Litman, and Farberow,

(1992) used this construct to assist the Los Angeles medical examiner's office in deciding whether the death of a 46-year-old male who had fallen off a pier into the ocean should be adjudicated as an accident or a suicide. The first completed psychological autopsy was a community-based study of 134 consecutive suicides occurring between 1956-1957 in St. Louis. Since that time, only a handful of these studies have been conducted. According to Clark (1992, p. 144), "these studies have made unique and significant contributions to the clinician's understanding of completed suicide." He is right, but a few issues must be considered.

First of all, these studies are limited methodologically. In any given year we lose approximately 30,000 to 35,000 individuals to suicide. There has never been, nor will there ever be, the capacity to evaluate the entire population of men and women who die by suicide. So the research is based on a small, representative sample of completed suicides. Moreover, this psychological autopsy method relies on information gathered from "knowledgeable informants" who may present subjective information to the interviewer. Research methods are designed to reduce or eliminate the subjectivity of the informant's reports. However, their validity can never be totally relied upon, because validity is based on replicated information, with numerous studies revealing identical, or near-identical, results. The bottom line: Studies on suicide are a challenge. That being said, let us now examine what these psychological autopsies have revealed about the psychological, behavioral, psychiatric, social, academic, occupational, vocational, relational, and other factors that are correlated to completed suicides.

CHAPTER ONE

Risk Factors For
Completed Suicide

A n essential theme that will be repeated throughout this book is: Suicide is, perhaps, the ultimate individualized experience. Shneidman commented years ago at a conference I was attending that, "you can have a hundred suicidal folks in a room, and for each one of those people there will be a different pathway to their suicide." Shneidman continuously reminded us that this "psychache" that he spoke of was "individually defined." He reminds us that, "one person's unbearable agony is another person's irksome event." There is no universal definition of the suicide event. It is an event specific to each individual. That being said, let us now examine some of the common risk factors that studies have revealed are experienced by the individual early in the suicide process. Such an examination of risk factors to suicide is essential. These are conditions that create in a person a vulnerability to see suicide as an attractive problem-solving strategy. They are often called "early warning signs." The essential point here is: This is the clinician's usual point of intervention. Early intervention is the key, and this is the clinician's signal for early intervention. When these risk factors are observed in a clinical setting the therapist is urged to pursue gentle, respectful probing into the patient's possible suicidal thoughts. These risk factors are grouped into three categories: 1) Psychiatric disorders, 2) Social stressors, 3) Psychological vulnerabilities.

Psychiatric Disorders

Dysthymia

This is a very low key, subtle, insidious, chronic depressive disorder. It can begin in adolescence and, if undiagnosed and untreated can continue for a person's life. One of the problems with this condition is that because of its subtle nature people eventually become, syntonic to its effect. They will often claim, "Well...this is just the way I am." And, therefore, they are at risk of not seeking treatment for this easily treated disorder. These are functional people. They are involved in vocational activities, occupational activities, relationships, social activities.

These patients present clinically as tired, lethargic, having little energy, no enthusiasm nor passion about life. When this clinical observation is made over a period of time, interventions are called for. For the most part, dysthymia is not disabling. In an interview on National Public Radio, the writer Hunter S. Thompson, who died a few months later by suicide, stated," I've never been disabled by depression. I've always been quite functional. I've just always felt a certain disconnect from my life." This statement was, possibly, a metaphor for dysthymia. Our clients give us information about themselves through metaphors. Readers are urged to pay attention to the metaphors our clients give to us. It may be their invitation to us to pursue more information about them.

It is important to note here—and it was the case with Thompson—that individuals with dysthymia often self-medicate with alcohol. What they discover when under the influence of alcohol and, in some cases, opioids and cocaine is a transient relief from the symptoms of this subtle depressive disorder. They find alcohol provides them with energy, enthusiasm, passion. They become social, they engage in conversations, they can become "the life of the party." Those of you who work with men and women with alcohol-related issues remain alert to metaphors such as: "people like me better when I'm drunk." This could reveal alcohol as a very attractive relief from the symptoms of dysthymia. Of essential importance here is that dysthymics frequently become the "self-medicating mentally ill." They become men and women with comorbid depressive and substance-related disorders—a major correlate to completed suicide. Studies by Klerman (1987) revealed that "the interaction of substance abuse and depression is an especially lethal combination." Cornelius, Salloum and Mezznich (1995) found that suicide was more common in patients with co-occurring depression and alcohol dependence when compared to patients with either disorder alone.

The essential question we must ask of all men and women with substance-related disorders is: "what does the drug do for you?" Listen to their responses and pay close attention to any metaphor giving a sense of the drug being used for relief from a medical mental disorder. Remember that all behaviors are purposeful. Many of our patients with substance-related disorders are finding their drug helpful in giving them temporary relief from the symptoms of an undiagnosed and untreated mood disorder. Hunter S. Thompson proclaimed during his NPR interview that he was "at my most creative while intoxicated." He died by suicide three months after that interview.

The chronic nature of dysthymia adds to the risk of suicide in this population. If it is allowed to go on long enough without intervention and treatment it could become correlated to *hopelessness.* Listen for metaphors for hopelessness as it is an essential ingredient for a completed suicide. Shneidman called it one of the "commonalities of suicide." My take on it: Suicide cannot occur outside of the mindset of hopelessness. Suicide is the direct result of hopelessness.

Many years ago I met a 49-year-old woman who was referred to me by her husband. He reported that since the recent wedding of their oldest daughter his wife had become "very depressed and was talking about wanting to die." As I began to know her she presented a clinical picture of chronic fatigue, tiredness, and lack of energy. She also delivered metaphors of having a very "boring life." She then said, "When our oldest daughter announced her engagement I thought to myself, 'here's my chance to experience some happiness, to be engaged in something.'" She then went on to say, "But it did absolutely nothing for me." And then she added, "If I can't be happy at my daughter's wedding, when will I ever experience happiness?" A metaphor, it turned out, for hopelessness, which was directly correlated to her undiagnosed, untreated dysthymia. Medication was prescribed, talking therapy continued, and she did quite well.

Major Depression, Recurrent, Severe, With Psychotic Features

While Major Depressive disorder increases the risk of suicide, this specific diagnosis, with these specifiers, is the major correlate to completed suicide. It is recommended that when we have a client with this diagnosis or demonstrating behaviors associated with this diagnosis we approach them as having a medical disorder from which they could die. It is that important. Perhaps no other medical mental disorder is more powerfully correlated to suicide than this diagnosis. This is disabling depression. These individuals are greatly challenged in vocational, occupational pursuits and have significant difficulty in relationships and social interactions.

This issue has been the subject of research since 1933: the year that all states were required to begin reporting suicide-related data to the Centers for Disease Control. From my readings and experience, the most influential research has been that conducted by Clark. His psychological autopsy studies have consistently revealed that major depressive disorder "is implicated as one pivotal factor in 40 to 60 percent of all (studied) completed suicides by adults."(Clark, 1992) But, he points out that since 1945 the suicide rate in the U.S. has remained relatively consistent (between ten and 13 per 100,000 individuals) while the incidence of major depression has climbed considerably. He suggests that the role of better access to mental health services, antidepressant medication, and mood stabilizers could explain this paradox.

Major depression, while a powerful correlate to completed suicide, is NOT causal. There is no universal way to explain a suicide. Years ago Shneidman warned: "I have noticed a disturbing trend in suicide prevention," he said. "I fear we have medicalized suicide and medicinalized its cure." He warned us and we have not been paying attention. What he was saying is that we cannot reduce suicide to merely the outcome of a medical mental disorder. And, most important, we cannot allow ourselves to believe that medication and its appropriate administration is the "cure" to suicide. He consistently stresses to us that suicide is a COMPLEXITY. Is the administration of medication an essential adjunct in the overall treatment of the suicidal patient? It certainly is. What Shneidman was saying was that when it becomes the ONLY focus of treatment we are going down a dangerous path.

Bipolar Disorders

Bipolar disorders are significantly correlated to suicide when accurately diagnosed. Goodwin and Jamison (1990) revealed in their studies that 20 percent of men and women with severe bipolar disorders die by suicide. But act cautiously in this arena. Accurate diagnosis is essential in determining suicide risk with this diagnosis. I have had clients come into my practice proclaiming to have a "bipolar disorder." When I explore with them which of the bipolar disorders they have been diagnosed with they stare at me in total bewilderment. I will usually send them back to their diagnostician for an accurate diagnosis. Claiming a person has a bipolar disorder tells me nothing about risk for suicide. I must be able to differentiate between Bipolar I and Bipolar II for an accurate risk assessment.

Bipolar Disorders are classified in the *Diagnostic and Statistical Manual of Mental Disorders IV-Text Revision* (DSM-IV-TR) as Bipolar I, Bipolar II, and Cyclothymic disorder. Risk for suicide demands accurate diagnostics. Studies by Dunner, Gershon and Goodman (1976), Stallone Dunner, Ahearn and Fieve (1980), and Rihmer, Barsi, Arata and Demeter (1990) reveal that Bipolar II disorder carries the highest risk for suicide. The latter study examined over 100 consecutive suicides in patients with mood disorders. It was found that 46 percent had Bipolar II disorder, 53 percent had Major Depressive disorder, and 1 percent had Bipolar I disorder.

Psychotic Grandiosity instead of hypomania

Bipolar I disorder is perhaps the most devastating of the bipolar disorders. But it appears, from research conducted by Reich and Winokur (1969), Robins, Murphy and Wilkinson (1959), and Weeke and Vaeth (1999), to carry a very low risk for suicide. Some reasons? Here is a diagnosis: Bipolar I disorder Most Recent Episode Manic, Severe, with Psychotic Features that are Mood Congruent. What does this diagnosis mean? It means that the person has met the criteria for Bipolar I disorder in the manic phase due to psychotic levels of grandiosity. They are currently involved in grandiose schemes: developing the cure to cancer, writing the next great American novel, sailing across the Atlantic in a bathtub—and all of this to be done by tomorrow afternoon! They are having the time of their lives. They are having more fun than anyone should be allowed to have and they are very important people, often referring to themselves as the second coming of the Deity. This psychotic grandiosity can actually prevent their suicides because they are too vital and important to die. This manic phase could actually act as a suicide preventative. *grandiosity* Except that their impaired judgment may cause them to die by accident. They are vulnerable to significant risk-taking behavior during this phase and this should be the primary concern. Also of concern during this phase is that this would be the period of time for non-compliance with medication, which will likely exacerbate the illness and lead to possible life-threatening consequences. The depressive phase of Bipolar I disorder is associated with a greatly disproportionate rate of suicide. What is even more interesting, however, is Weeke and Vaeth's finding that nearly 30 percent of suicide victims were classified as being in a "depressive state, recovering" at the time of death (1999). There are several hypotheses that may account for the observation that many individuals take their lives not when they are in the depths of depression but when they seem to be getting better. This improvement may be associated with a subtle "return to energy" or "just enough energy to take their lives" and a lack of sufficient energy when the depression is at its worst. ✶

This hypothesis also accounts for the observation that the majority of bipolar suicides occur with Bipolar II disorder. The differential between Bipolar I and Bipolar II is the manic phase. In Bipolar II disorder the manic phase is referred to as "hypomania" or a subtle return to energy rather than the psychotic grandiosity seen in Bipolar I disorder. Patients with Bipolar I disorder With Rapid Cycling, who may cycle in a short period between full-blown mania and depression are also at increased risk for suicide. Schweizer, Dever and Clary (1988) discovered that the "rapid cycling mood" is associated with increased risk for completed suicide.

A final word on the issue of suicide with the bipolar population that appears to reflect the findings noted above. Let me tell you a story: A number of years ago I had periodic clinical contact with gentleman diagnosed with Bipolar I disorder. He was in his mid-40s, had been diagnosed in his early 20s, and had a long history of non-compliance with his medication. At the time of this story he was in the midst of a manic episode. Finally, he was captured, taken to Probate Court, and was placed in a psychiatric facility for a court-ordered evaluation. While he was in this protective environment he was reintroduced to his medication. He began to stabilize, his symptoms remitted, and he became more alert. At this time he realized the havoc he had brought upon himself during the manic phase. He discovered that he had a sexually transmitted disease for which there was no cure due to excessive, unprotected sex during his mania. He discovered that he had acquired an addiction to cocaine during his mania. He discovered that he was in thousands of dollars in debt due to irresponsible financial dealings during his mania. He discovered that his spouse had left him and filed for divorce and that he had lost his job. He discovered all of this on a psychiatric unit while he was "improving." Two days after coming to these realizations about his damaged life, he was found dead by strangulation in his room. He appears to be the classic bipolar suicide. Clinicians are reminded to be alert to these "improvements" and to be certain to discover what the client may have experienced during his or her manic episode. If it is found that they brought considerable havoc to their lives that should encourage close observation on the unit and very specific and comprehensive discharge plans, with detailed social and community supports.

Generalized Anxiety Disorder

This is a tricky diagnostic category. It has a certain "downside" in that these people are always worried, in crisis, and agitated. But, this disorder also has an "upside." They are often productive, highly energized citizens, and/or workaholics. They are often seen as perfectionists where they attend to every detail in accomplishing a task. They will often use their "productivity" to manage the symptoms of their generalized anxiety by being constantly busy. But the bottom line is that these folks can't relax. They are constantly worried, constantly busy, they can't tolerate vacuums, and they can't experience peace, tranquility, or calmness. And in states of high anxiety they drive support systems to avoid them.

Like the dysthymic individual, clients with Generalized Anxiety disorder often self-medicate—in this case primarily with cannabis. Again, the question to ask is: "what does marijuana do for you?" Be alert to metaphors such as, "when I'm stoned I don't have a worry in the world" or "it's the only way I can chill." As the self-medicating mentally ill, these individuals should be considered at risk for suicide.

Posttraumatic Stress Disorder (PTSD)

This mental health issue has been seen as a significant risk factor for suicide and self-mutilation for years. Our knowledge of this disorder has increased over the years to give us ample insights into the treatment and care of this population. Research by Loftus, Polonsky, and Fullilove (1994), suggests that patients will often develop other Axis I disorders as methods of "coping" with the disturbing symptoms of this condition. Substance use disorders, eating disorders, somatization disorders, and dissociative disorders are common concurrent diagnoses of individuals struggling with this primary disorder. Accordingly, PTSD has often been termed an "umbrella disorder" as it often "covers" or incorporates numerous comorbid conditions. This comorbidity increases the suicide risk in this population. Herman (1992) and Gold (2000) alert us to the significance of the "developmental complex trauma disorder" where the individual's exposure to trauma was not an isolated, terrorizing event, but a persistent, chronic exposure to abuse or pain. Research by Linehan (1999) urges us to be alert to this "developmental complex" form of PTSD that is quite often observed in men and women with the diagnosis of Borderline Personality disorder and a history of chronic abuse. She alerts us to the extreme vulnerability of this population to self-mutilation and suicide.

Schizophrenia

Approximately 90 percent of men and women who die by suicide, and who have been studied through psychological autopsies, were shown to have had a psychiatric illness at the time of their death (Barraclough, 1974). Of those, between 45 and 70 percent, depending on the study, had a mood disorder such as major depression or a bipolar disorder. Between two and twelve percent had schizophrenia at the time of their death (Black, 1990). It is estimated by Roy (1995) that 10 to 15 percent of men and women with schizophrenia will die by suicide. But, the most remarkable feature of this population is that the majority of them are in a depressive state, rather than a psychotic state, at the time of their suicide. The lethal combination of schizophrenia and an underlying, often undetected and untreated, depression should command the clinician's respect.

Many years ago I knew a young psychiatrist—a talented diagnostician and therapist—who would routinely give all of her patients with schizophrenia anti-depressant medication along with the anti-psychotic meds "just in case" there was an underlying depressive disorder that she could not detect at the time due to the overt nature of the psychotic symptoms.

Research also shows (Noreik, 1984) that the paranoid and disorganized subtype of schizophrenia is at the highest risk for premature death and vicious forms of self-mutilation. We are all urged to be alert to the behaviors described as "responding to internal stimuli." It is a reminder that a patient could be hallucinations/Delusions experiencing auditory hallucinations. We should always ask patients who are distracted, laughing or talking to themselves (responding to internal stimuli) whether they are hearing voices. If they respond affirmatively to that question, we then ask them, "what are the voices saying to you?" If they give us any metaphor for what is termed "command, persecutory" hallucinations, e.g., "they are telling me that my eye is evil and I should pluck it out," we must respond immediately with in-patient safety and a review of current meds. This feature of "command, persecutory" hallucinations is a significant warning sign for horrible forms of self-mutilation. These patients will respond to these hallucinations—plucking out eyes, cutting off hands, self-castration—in the hope that responding to the voices will quiet them. Men and women with schizophrenia are vulnerable to premature death during such delusional states.

Many years ago I was involved in the death investigation of a young man in his mid-40s who tragically died after jumping from his seventh floor apartment. The county medical examiner ruled his death a suicide and, as a result, his insurance policy refused to distribute funds from a rather significant death benefit. The family filed suit against the insurance carrier. For a death to be ruled a suicide on a death certificate it is necessary for the deceased to have displayed, prior to the death, that the activity they were engaging in had the intent of terminating their existence. You cannot have a suicide without the intent to die. Prior to his death he was experiencing an internalized delusion of being "Superman"—he became someone he was not. He was often seen wearing his blue tee-shirt with an "S" painted on it and a red blanket as a "cape." His fellow residents in the apartment building teased and ridiculed him for this "delusion." One day he reportedly decided that he was going to prove to his fellow residents that he was, indeed, "Superman." He took some of his friends up to his apartment, opened up the window, and jumped.

The one thing we know about Superman is that he can fly. Because of his impaired judgment at that time, this young man believed he would fly and his "intent" when he jumped was to prove to his doubting friends that he was, indeed, capable of this feat. His tragic death, therefore, did not meet the criterion of intent, and the ruling of suicide was very appropriately challenged by the family. The bottom line was that this young man died during a delusional state. We need to be ever-alert with men and women with psychotic disorders and their demonstrated hallucinations and delusions. These active symptoms of psychosis put a person at significant risk for both self-mutilation and accidental death.

Studies by Roy (1990) and Virkkunen (1996) reveal to us that young males with schizophrenia are at elevated risk for suicide. They claim that this group's vulnerability to suicide is "exceptional." Sheidman (1985) claimed that suicide in this group appears to be "an attempt to extricate oneself from an intolerable life situation." Williams, Dalby, Kumar, Prasad, and Dassori (1992) place an emphasis on the role of **hopelessness** in the suicides of young men with this disorder. This hopelessness comes, quite often, from the stigma of this particular mental illness in our society which frequently makes life intolerable for these individuals. Their fear is that the diagnosis of schizophrenia represents the end of their life dreams, expectations, and hopes. For those of you who work with this population it is of vital importance to capture from the recently diagnosed individual with schizophrenia his or her emotional reaction to this diagnosis—and listen for metaphors for hopelessness. Finally, due to the significant genetic issues involved in this mental disorder, those of you who work with adolescents should always ask them, primarily at intake, "do you have a history of mental illness in your family?" Many adolescents will not know the answer to this question, but ask it regardless. A positive response is a signal to pay even closer attention to the evaluation of that client. Schizophrenia in the male normally emerges between the ages of 17 and 24. In the female it will emerge somewhat later, between the ages of 26 and 32. It should be emphasized that the earlier the diagnosis, the more effective is our ability to capture issues of hopelessness in this vulnerable population.

Substance-Related Disorders

As previously noted, the self-medicating mentally ill are at increased risk of death by suicide. I want to begin by discussing the Hopeless Addict. These are people who cannot see their lives without their drug. Their entire realm of functioning involves the acquisition and use of drugs. Vocational, occupational, relational or social activities are secondary to, or are incorporated into, their pursuit of drugs. They are individuals who will typically present with the diagnosis of "substance dependence." The primary goal of their drug use is to avoid withdrawal symptoms. They are often involved in the criminal justice system when their history of use has resulted in social, relational, vocational, or occupational disasters. I remember a man telling me once during a session: "Telling me to quit cocaine is like telling me to stop breathing." The drug became essential for him to continue functioning. These patients will frequently present under coercion...or in a stage of high "resistance." Their risk for suicide is significant due to their vulnerability to hopelessness. Their view is that the only way out of this "living hell" they have found themselves in is to die. What are some of the specific predictors of suicide in this population?

Their drug use began, more often than not, during adolescence as a method of managing an undetected, undiagnosed, untreated mood, anxiety, and/or psychotic disorder. They experienced significant childhood pathology. Their history of drug use has resulted in significant losses in relationships, vocational and occupational opportunities, deteriorating physical health, involvement in the justice system, and significant damage to self-esteem. They have a lessened sense of autonomy (literally becoming prisoners of their drug) and display high levels of self-criticism and self-hate. Studies (Murphy, Davidson, and Slattery, 2003) have added to these predictors: History of polysubstance dependence, significant elements of sociopathy, multiple treatment failures and relapse history, significant history of familial drug use, more often from broken homes and victims of child abuse. My own experience with this population is wrought with alarm and concern. I have experienced a number of at-risk groups in my 45-year career…but none are more at risk than the dually diagnosed patients at the extreme end of this spectrum—the realm of the "hopeless addict." I urge all readers to be especially attentive to this population. There was a time when the prognosis for this population was dismal to say the least. But recent advances in treatment from Ken Minkoff, MD at Case Western Reserve University, and Donald Meichenbaum, Ph.D. at the University of Waterloo, Ontario, Canada have given us hope that many of these patients may eventually gain autonomy, control, and have a life worth living.

Summary

David Clark (1992) made an interesting comment years ago when he said: "suicide never occurs outside of the context of a mental illness." While we always want to be cautious when we hear words like "never" and "always," he was right on target. As mentioned earlier, studies on completed suicides have revealed that 90 percent, 93 percent, and 95 percent, respectively, experienced at their death: a mood disorder, anxiety, or psychosis often times complicated by a co-occurring substance-related disorder. What is of further concern is that out of this 90+ percent we know that 70 percent were experiencing a depressive disorder at the time of their suicide. All of this information is a powerful reminder to respect that those clients we see who are experiencing these issues should be considered *at risk* for suicide and should be approached accordingly.

Social Stressors

Suicide never occurs outside of the context of major social stressors. Clinicians are consistently advised to be on alert for the client who presents with numerous burdensome, challenging stressors. Epidemiology has given us, over the years, ample information about the pronounced social stressors which are correlated risk factors to completed suicide. Importantly, these stressors are very specific to certain groups and populations. What may be a stressor for an adolescent female may not be an issue with an elderly male. We are also aware of the fact that different cultural populations have their own idiosyncratic stressors. This underscores the need to view stress from a cultural, gender, age, vocational, occupational perspective which will respect the nuances of individual groups. We will do our best, in this effort, to give the reader information on the stressors related to suicide in specific groups.

Adult

Stressors correlated to suicide in this population will be categorized under "issues of loss." Discovering the losses that your adult client has experienced within a recent time frame is of extreme importance when evaluating vulnerability to suicide. From a broad perspective the following are the issues of loss we need to be attentive to:

Loss of Primary Relationships. Discovering in our client any sense of aloneness, abandonment, rejection, isolation should be a primary focus during an evaluation session. The adult female and the elderly male are extremely vulnerable to suicide under these conditions. Special attention must be given to the adult client who demonstrates behaviors associated with Borderline Personality disorder, or with borderline features, such as issues of abandonment and isolation/rejection, are psychologically intolerable for this population. The borderline patient may use forms of self-mutilation to regulate the terror of being alone or may be suicide-vulnerable when using drugs to cope with aloneness. Theories from Linehan (1993), Gunderson (1985), and Fonagy (1997) speak volumes about the risk that isolation/ rejection brings to this special population.

In the elderly male, aloneness is usually a result of the death of a life partner and the challenge of facing the remaining years without that intimate connection. Pay special attention, however, when that loss is due to a suicide. Survivors of suicide have a horrible task in their grieving process and are often vulnerable to suicidal ideation themselves.

Loss of Health. It is well established that chronic medical disorders present a vulnerability to suicide. Multiple Sclerosis, cancer of the brain, HIV/AIDS, renal failure, Parkinson's or Huntington's disease with comorbidities such as depression, alcohol addiction, psychosis, and/or advanced age are clearly correlated to risk for suicide. Also remain alert to traumatic brain and spinal injuries with comorbid conditions of depression, drug use, anxiety, and violent acting-out. At issue here is the patient's loss of autonomy and control, dependency on others, damage to self-image, and collateral issues of loss of financial security, and social and occupational definition.

Loss of Social Definition. I remember a young man, in his mid-40s, telling me during a session: "nobody out there gives me a thought." Abject, total, complete sense of aloneness is oftentimes more profoundly painful than the loss of a primary relationship. We are, after all, social beings. With the dramatic exception of the Schizoid Personality disorder, we yearn for social connection. Without this element in our lives we can experience emotional and intellectual decay. I am sure that many of you who are reading this have met men and women who will, literally, do **anything** to get this connectedness. They will engage, often, in behaviors that we may view as dysfunctional, maladaptive, pathological. But for them, at this period in their lives, these behaviors are essential to keep them alive. The term, "bonding through Budweiser" refers to men and women who use alcohol to gain this connectedness. How often have I heard from clients with alcohol issues: "My best friends are the guys I hang out with at my favorite watering hole…thank heavens for them, they make life OK." We need to be alert and aware that some of our clients' apparently maladaptive behaviors are actually behaviors that prevent them from becoming suicidal.

Loss of Occupational Definition. This is *not* job loss. Job loss and unemployment are devastating, but are not necessarily correlated to suicide. We are talking here about people who define themselves by what they do for a living. Quite simply, they are what they do. Their entire self-concept is formed through performance and when that performance is interrupted or lost they will experience intolerable damage to their self-image. We know that the elderly (65+) white male has an exceptionally elevated risk for suicide, and one of the contributors to that risk is retirement. As I write this book I am retired and in my mid-60s. I have a friend who after about seven months of retirement went back to work. Why? Financial concerns? No! As he said to me one evening: "I need a reason to get up in the morning." Of special concern with this population is when loss of occupational definition is coupled with severe threat to financial security, loss of social definition, and damage to self-esteem. Finally, under this category we want to address a special focus on the "extra-familial murder-suicide." This population usually comprises disgruntled individuals with significant issues of paranoia and narcissism who view their loss of occupational definition as a significant rejection and humiliation. Their act of murder-suicide is directed at those who have "wronged" them. The primary goal here is murder. The suicide is an avoidance of consequences.

Many of us work with special populations who, because of their dynamics, run a significant risk of experiencing these types of losses. It is important to be aware that certain groups, e.g., men and women with substance-related disorders, severe, persistent mental disorders, the incarcerated and the elderly have a certain vulnerability to experiencing these stressors.

Adolescent

While the adolescent population will experience similar reactions to the adult stressors we have discussed, they have their own stressors that should be respected. While there will be overlap in these stressors, the adolescent will experience them in different ways and with different levels of intensity than the adult.

Substance-Related Disorders for Self-Management. Like adults, adolescents with undetected, undiagnosed, untreated emerging mental disorders are highly likely to experiment with substances. The self-medicating mentally ill dynamic begins in adolescence. This is due to the fact that the majority of mental illnesses emerge in adolescence. Many of our teens will find or discover in drugs a temporary relief from the symptoms of depression, anxiety, or psychosis. As always, it is essential for those of us who work with the adolescent who uses drugs to ask the question, *"what does the drug do for you?"* Listen carefully to any direct or metaphoric response that gives a hint that the drug use is attractive to the adolescent because it provides him or her with transient relief from these emerging mental disorders. They find in cannabis relief from anxiety; they find in alcohol relief from depression, they find in cocaine relief from depression. Remember that the self-medicating mentally ill have a significant vulnerability to suicide. The best intervention is early intervention. The best opportunity to effectively intervene in this pattern of drug use is in its early stages.

Aloneness/Isolation. Rejection and aloneness are intolerable to many adolescents. Those of you who work with this group know that they will do anything to avoid isolation and aloneness and that this desperate need often motivates some of the maladaptive behaviors that bring young people to our offices. An essential question that must be asked of all adolescents during an evaluation period is: "Tell me about your friends." Listen to their metaphors.

Many years ago I met a 17-year-old young man who was referred by a drug court after he received his second DUI. When he came to my attention he was addicted to alcohol, cocaine, and cannabis. He was a self-mutilator, had significant suicidal ideation, and had been involved in the juvenile justice system in his area since he was 12 years old. He was also in a significant state of resistance and denial. A rather typical adolescent referral! During our initial intake session I asked him: "Tell me about your friends." His response: "Not much to say with that. We're just a bunch of guys who get together at night in the park. We drink and get rowdy together." I then asked him: "Is there anything else you guys do together other than drink and get rowdy?" He gave me a look that said, "you are dumb as a bag of rocks." But, he then said to me: "I don't even know their names." And then he added, giving me the most profound metaphor for aloneness I've heard in my 45-year career: "You know, man, when I die they're going to be able to hold my funeral in a phone booth." Remember earlier when I advised that we don't treat behaviors, we treat people. Remember that Edwin Shneidman told us earlier that the first task of therapy is to identify the locus of the client's unbearable pain and to decrease the perturbation associated with that condition. That young man gave me a gift that day. It was a gift that I could not morally or ethically ignore. He was sent to my office by the drug court for substance use counseling. He was not, however, invested in that focus. Where he hurt, the locus of his pain, was abject isolation. All of his maladaptive behaviors were in reaction to his core element of pain—his aloneness. Edwin Shneidman called it: the "psychache." The drug court had given me six sessions for that young man; he stayed with me for over two years. He never missed a session. Why? He gave me a gift and I accepted the gift and, in doing so, I gave him ownership of the therapy experience.

Victim of Bullying. Zero tolerance. Bullying is significantly correlated with adolescent suicide as it triggers themes of abandonment, isolation, rejection, and devaluation. Zero tolerance...enough said.

Acculturation Issues. It has been recognized for years that our gay, lesbian, bisexual, transgender adolescents are vulnerable to suicidal ideation and suicide attempts (Muehrer, (1991). There are no studies at present however indicating a higher rate of completed suicides. They appear at risk for attempts and ideation when they experience a message of rejection from primary support systems because of their sexual orientation.

Attention must be paid also to adolescents of other cultures. Goldston (2008) presents a framework for considering the cultural context of suicidal behavior in specific racial, ethnic, cultural groups: African American, Asian American, Native American, and Latino adolescents. This research is on the cutting edge of the movement in psychology to respect the diversity of our society and move away from the "white male" perspective.

Academic Performance Anxiety. Adolescents who believe that affirmation and love are won and earned are vulnerable. Love is not freely given. The adolescent who believes that love is earned through performance is at risk. They receive a message that they are only loved for what they do; they are not loved for who they are. Academic achievement is often a focus of this performance that teens use to gain affirmation and love from their primary support system. Problem—what is won and earned can be lost. The issue with these young people is they have no capacity to psychologically manage failure. Academic failure (and a B+ can be a failure) is intolerable, because it means a loss of love. This is one of the major contributors to suicide ideation, attempts, and completion on a college campus or in a high school setting.

Family Discord. A chaotic home environment greatly enhances an adolescent's vulnerability to suicide. Issues such as witnessing substance use and/or spousal assault in the home, being victimized by sexual, physical, emotional assault, issues of rejection, abandonment and neglect all contribute to an adolescent's despair, robbing him or her of a sense of safety, and self-worth. A vital question to be asked of all adolescents during an evaluation process: "How are things at home?" Caution is advised around the adolescent who responds to that question with glowing, almost unrealistic, qualities attributed to the primary caregivers. That adolescent is often seen as vulnerable to "keeping the big secret." There is something wrong in that home and the adolescent appears to be compensating by making his parents sound like the second coming of Ward and June Cleaver! Teens who come from wonderful homes typically find something wrong with Mom or Dad…it's in their DNA to do this. So caution is advised with the teen who appears to go "over the top" with praise for his/her primary support.

Impulsivity and Access to Firearms. Adolescents are impulsive. Describing the impulsive adolescent is describing the adolescent who walks and breathes simultaneously. Why is this their burden?

They do not have wisdom. Wisdom comes with age. It comes with life experiences. It is the result of our ability to pay attention to life's lessons. The 13-year-old boy who has just been tragically dumped by the "love of his life" is now experiencing an extreme degree of psychological turmoil—possibly for the first time in his life. Since he has not acquired the wisdom of experience he does not know that this pain will eventually decrease, maybe even go away in just a short time. He is not yet aware of any coping or problem-solving strategies to manage this pain and, therefore, at this time in his life there appears to be no way to effectively deal with this turmoil. That very same pain as experienced by a 45-year-old male who has "been down this road before" is not going to be life threatening because he has experience with this kind of thing. He knows it will get better and he knows how to cope because of life experiences.

But, that 13-year-old just happens to live in a home that has access to firearms and, in an impulsive moment, he makes the devastating decision to use a gun to end his existence and, in so doing, end his pain. It is important for those of you who work with adolescents to ask them during intake: "Do you have access to firearms in your home?" If the adolescent responds in the affirmative to that question we are then encouraged to call the primary caregiver and respectfully and professionally request that they make the firearm, that the adolescent currently sees as accessible, inaccessible. We are NOT asking them to "rid" the home of firearms. That approach may create unproductive defensiveness. We merely want them to make all firearms in the home "safe" from impulsive use. Most primary caregivers will respond positively to that request. If, however, you receive an inappropriate amount of refusal on the part of the primary caregiver your next step is to file a report with your local Child Protective Services agency on "child endangerment" grounds. Your job in this area is now done; you have clearly exercised your mandate in a responsible fashion.

I would add here, as we conclude our discussion on adolescent stressors, to be attentive to the adolescent who has lost a loved one or a "significant person" to suicide. They experience the complex grief of the adult, but they also may view that suicide as a "role model" for "problem solving."

Child

Debates rage as to whether children are capable of dying by suicide. From a forensic position these debates are quite entertaining. What we are concerned about is that children are vulnerable to "premature death." In suicide studies we often find children and adolescents placed together, and distinctions are made between the two groups only in a subtle fashion. Children who have suicide ideation, have attempted suicide, or have completed suicide are not a homogeneous group, which makes a broad understanding of this group quite difficult. Suicidal thoughts or acts have intense individual meanings and purposes that can be understood only in the context of the individual child's life. What I have discovered in my career, and is reinforced in some studies, children are vulnerable to premature death under two primary stressors: *loss of a love object* and *hopelessness*.

Loss of a Love Object. The concern here is the grieving child and their under-developed, immature perception of the finality of death. Many years ago I had the distinct privilege of meeting the youngest client in my 45-year career. He was seven years old. He was in my office, because, the day before, thankfully, he was observed by a school guard as he crouched under the wheels of the school bus right before the bus was to leave the school parking lot. The guard rushed into action and dragged the little boy out from under the bus just before it left the lot. A few minutes later and this little boy most surely would have been killed. As he was taken by the guard back to the building, he was screaming at the guard to let him go so he could "go see my Daddy." In the school building, as he was being interviewed by every adult present, he remained upset at the guard and proclaimed to everyone present that he "just wanted to see Daddy" and "I'll be back at school tomorrow." What was this little boy's experience? Two weeks prior to this event, this little boy had lost his best friend— his father who had died from a heart attack at the age of 34 one afternoon while he was mowing the lawn. In the family's understandable, spiritually-focused message of hope they told him: "Daddy is dead, he is in Heaven with God, and we will see him when we die." An understandable, spiritually-based message with one major flaw—not understanding the immature perspective of the finality of death in children. In this message this little boy heard: "Daddy is still alive, in a place called Heaven, with a person named God, and we will see him when we die." It is important to maintain this hope in the face of the death of a loved one. But the message for children must also include a perspective of the finality of death. In children there should be a focus on: death being the end of life as this individual child experiences it. So, in the clinical experience we invite the child's mother and grandparents into session to experience the grieving together, as a family. And in this process we get to know this little boy. We become intimate with special aspects of his life, and periodically convey the message that "death is the end of life as he, as an individual, experiences it." This frame results in periodic messages to this little boy: "Brian, when you die, you and Polly will never ride the school bus together again;" "Brian, when you die, you and Billy will never play together again;" "Brian, when you die, you never visit grandma and grandpa at their cottage by the lake ever again." Death is framed as the end of life as it is individually experienced by the child.

A final word on this important issue: Being the father of five children I have grown very fond over the years of the production "Sesame Street" by the Children's Television Workshop. A number of years ago this wonderful production company developed the "Family Guide to Grieving Resource Packet." For those of you who work with the grieving child, it is an essential.

Hopelessness. The reader, perhaps, recalls at the beginning of this work how I stressed the issue of *hopelessness* which is the primary fueling emotion to suicide. A suicide cannot occur without hopelessness. Suicide is the direct result of hopelessness, fatalistic despair. Later on in this book we will discuss the essential of listening for metaphors for hopelessness in our clients as a primary warning sign for suicide. The concern here: Children and their vulnerability to becoming hopeless. We often don't think of children and hopelessness in the same frame. After all, they have their whole lives in front of them, how could they become hopeless? But children do have a significant vulnerability to hopelessness and we must be aware of the factors that are conducive to its development.

Future time perspective. I have mentioned that as I write this book I am in my mid-60s and I am currently drawing on my Social Security. It comes by direct deposit into my checking account on the third day of each month. As I am writing this section of the book the third of next month and the arrival of my next social security check is 24 days from now. Twenty-four days. Folks, 24 days is a blip on my screen. I can do 24 days standing on my head. It's like a few moments from now. Bottom line...the older you are the more rapid the pace of time becomes. Try telling a seven-year-old, however, that it's 24 more days until we visit Grandma and Grandpa. For a seven-year-old that same 24 days is an eternity. Because of this lack of future time perspective many of our children in abusive situations fear they are going to be in the abusive situation forever—never to be released from the pain and chaos. It is this sense that can lead to their despair and hopelessness. Pay attention to their metaphors for hopelessness, even in young children, as it is a significant risk factor for premature death in children.

And a final word on survivors of suicide. Always remain respectful of the unique pain in this population. In children, that pain could be compounded by guilt and a misguided sense of responsibility for the suicidal death of a love object. Pay very close attention to any sense you get from the child survivor of suicide that they feel some responsibility for the tragic death of their loved one.

Psychological Vulnerabilities

Suicide never occurs outside of the context of medical mental disorders and significant social stressors. These are your early warning signs for a person vulnerable to, and at risk for, suicide. Over the years, the question has been not "why suicide?" but "why some suicides?" Data reveals, for instance, that in any given year millions of people experience the pain of major depression— this significant risk factor for suicide. Out of those millions only a fraction die by suicide. What is fascinating is that when you look at the prevalence of risk factors to suicide, i.e., depression, anxiety, substance-related disorders, divorce, unemployment, bullying, loss of a love object and then examine the numbers of men and women with those issues who die by suicide we realize that suicide is, indeed, a very RARE event. Why them? That is often the question asked. And it is answered by examining deficiencies in coping and problem-solving. Dr. Shneidman notes that all suicides are marked by a life-long pattern of weak, faulty coping and problem-solving skills. It is this issue we want to examine as we discuss with you the *psychological vulnerabilities* that create a risk for suicide in certain populations. We will approach these vulnerabilities from three areas: Performance Anxiety; Emotional Constriction; and The Defenseless Personality.

Performance Anxiety. "I am only loved for what I do," a young woman proclaimed to me years ago during a session. "I want to be loved for who I am," she continued. As I got to know her, I discovered that her early years were spent in a "performance-oriented" home environment. The circumstances that brought her to my attention involved a highly concerning suicide attempt. She was 20 years old and in her sophomore year at a local four-year liberal arts college near the community where I practice. One evening the entire student body was in the college auditorium for an event. She was alone in her dorm dying from severe lacerations she had produced on both of her arms. Her roommate, who was in the auditorium, found she had forgotten her camera and came up to the dorm room to get it. She found my soon-to-be client lying on the floor in a pool of blood and immediately called for rescue.

Three weeks later this young lady was in my office for counseling. During our first few sessions she described her parents as "wonderful people." But she also described being subjected by them to significant expectations of performance that were subtly tied into receiving affirmation and love from them. During our third session, my client expressed a desire to have her parents involved in the counseling sessions. We invited the parents to join us and they agreed. My client was correct; they were, indeed, "wonderful people." But the expectations that she spoke of were demonstrated by the parents during our first session with them. The parents spoke of their hopes, wishes, and aspirations for their daughter. They went to great lengths to describe to me the "family plan." What was the family plan? The parents tell me: "The reason Lisa is at that college is because that is where her father and I went to school. We met at that school, and we got married in the school chapel. It is a wonderful place to get your college education. Lisa wanted to go to a state university and we would hear nothing of it," Mother explains. Father continues, "When Lisa gets her degree from that college she is then going to the law school that I attended to get her law degree. It is also where my father got his law degree." Mother continues, "When Lisa gets her law degree she is then going to join her father's law firm that was founded by her grandfather over 50 years ago. It is one of the most prestigious law firms in our state." Father then added. "When I retire, Lisa is going to become the managing partner of the firm, just as I became the managing partner when my father retired." And mother added, "And when Lisa retires we hope that one of her children will follow this path. We want this firm to always remain in the family." While the "family plan" was being unveiled to me, Lisa was in the corner of my office crying. The day she made her suicide attempt was the day that mid-term grades were released. On that day, she had received the very first "B" in her entire academic career. That night, in her mind, that "B" represented the end of the family plan and the intolerable result of losing her parents' love.

We are consistently reminded that suicide is an individual experience. There is no "golden key" that unlocks the reasons why men and women take their lives. As Shneidman reminds us: "One person's unbearable agony is another person's irksome event" (1985). This client's response to that grade was the perception that her parents "would no longer love me." For the first 20 years of her life she had received messages, subtle and overt, that parental love was dependent upon her responding to their expectations. To live without their approval and love was, for her, an unbearable agony. That "B" represented a failure. Clinicians need to be empathic to the client's interpretation of their lives. Our clients have the privilege of defining where they hurt and the locus of their pain. There is no codified manual of certified reasons why men and women become suicidal.

This story has a happy ending. These were, as I mentioned, wonderful parents who did, indeed, love this young woman. But they, also, labored under this "performance" issue that gave value to their lives. They worked hard to be "the best at everything." Failure was not an option for them in their personal lives. Once they discovered the focus of their daughter's suicide attempt, they were terrified. As therapy progressed, my client gained autonomy. She left the school of her parents' choice and went to the state university where she had wanted to go from the beginning. She did not go into law but instead found a profession that she had dreamed of since she was a little girl. And, most importantly, she remained loved by her parents as she made some decisions they did not particularly approve of.

Unconditional love is our desire. The need to be loved because we exist—with all of our flaws, poor decisions, and missteps—is a need we all have. John Bowlby in his wonderful 1988 book, *A Secure Base*, talks about how the therapist plays the role of the accepting parent. We accept our clients with all of their flaws and provide them with the empathic "secure base." Perfectionist qualities in a person can, sometimes, be quite admirable. These qualities can also kill us. When these qualities are reflective of the need to be loved and represent a sense that, "I can only be loved when I am perfect we could be looking at a person vulnerable to suicide. Therapists need to be aware of this issue and respectful of its risk.

Emotional Constriction. "You know" the young man in my office said to me, "I used to be proud of the fact that nothing I see bothers me anymore. I've been a cop for over 20 years and I've seen everything. I used to brag about it. Nothing affects me. I had to do this to do my job. You can't be a cop and feel. But I think this is killing me…I'm dead inside…I can't feel anything now." A week before I saw him he was discovered by a fellow officer sitting at his locker with a revolver in his mouth. He was divorced, estranged from his two children, living alone, no social context, and alcohol—dependent. His only friends were the folks he hung out with at the bar. He too "bonded through Budweiser." When he was intoxicated he became social, talkative, and humorous. When he was intoxicated he was free, temporarily, from this "dead inside" feeling. When he was intoxicated, he could "feel things." His use of alcohol was, literally, keeping him alive. His alcohol use gave him temporary relief from his dysthymia and also provided him with access to emotions that allowed him to stay alive. "You know," he went on to say, "people like me better when I'm drunk. I'm actually a pretty funny guy… when I'm drunk." He told me about his "jump-start breakfast"— two fingers neat of Jim Beam and a Budweiser chaser. It was his morning medication that allowed him to function during the day. He told me that his first destination after his shift was the bar. It was his safe haven. It was here that he "debriefed" after he had a few beers to make him "emotionally available."

His story was sad. He had chosen a profession that required suspension of emotions. There are a lot of those professions— oncology, emergency room medicine, law enforcement, military, EMS. He witnessed and vicariously experienced significant trauma in his job. He discovered that the only way to protect himself from the emotional onslaught of what he saw every day was to disconnect emotionally. He had to do this to do his job. He could not do his job and feel. But what was initially designed as a way to allow him to cope with his occupational pursuit, now became a pervasive element of his personality. He became emotionally constricted. He lost his capacity to experience emotional reactions. I remember during the initial stages of our relationship I would ask him how a certain event impacted on him from an emotional perspective, "how did that make you feel?" His response to that question was a blank stare. I would start reflecting emotions to him: "It must have been heartbreaking to see that." His response would be a blank stare. I would share my own emotional reaction: "Something like that would make me quite angry." His response would again be a blank stare. Without this capacity to be emotionally available, he began to lose relationships. It is difficult to develop and retain intimate relationships if you are not emotionally available. He became more and more alone. He became a person who self-medicated his depression, his aloneness, and his emotional constriction. He became seriously vulnerable to completed suicide.

This person was "invalidated" emotionally due to the demands of his profession. Many people are invalidated emotionally and, therefore, become emotionally constricted because of childhood experiences. Sometimes these invalidating messages we give to our children are subtle: "Quit the crying or I'll give you something to cry about;" "wipe that smile off your face;" "that's no reason to get angry." And sometimes these invalidating messages are pathological—sexual and/or physical abuse. One of the significantly damaging messages of abuse is: "I don't care how you feel; I'm going to do to you what I want to do to you. You can cry and scream all you want; I'm not going to stop. Your outbursts of emotion are useless." The result is the tragedy of emotional constriction—nobody knows how I feel. I am, indeed, alone.

The Defenseless Personality. Edwin Shneidman made a comment years ago that suicide is self-murder and that "one cannot kill what one loves; one can only kill what one hates." He presents to us a rather strong, but accurate, formulation of this terrible tragedy. This self-hate may be a temporary flash or a pervasive element of the self. The bottom line, however, is that the person believes that he or she is not capable of solving the problems life has thrown at them and they are inadequate to do anything effective to manage the unbearable level of pain they are now experiencing. They feel helpless.

I met a young woman a number of years ago who was in an internship at my practice as she pursued an advanced degree. She was brilliant—also, she was an excellent diagnostician and a wonderful clinician. She was going to be a gift to our profession. I noticed, however, that she didn't take praise and affirmation very well. She handled constructive criticism very nicely, but when I would quite often point out some excellent work she was doing with a client she would actually cringe. One day I brought this to her attention and she acknowledged that it was a characteristic of hers to "have a hard time with praise." I encouraged her to talk to someone about this issue since I feared it could interfere with a promising career. She followed through on my suggestion and often shared with me her self-discovery.

She had been sexually assaulted as a child. One of the more terrible effects of child abuse is that the abused child often incorporates the identity given to him or her by the predator. One of the more devastating messages given by the experience of child abuse is: "You are worthless." This sense of worthlessness became ingrained in her person as one of her personal demons. This sense of self often dictated how she thought, felt, behaved. The sense of "self-hate, self-devaluation, self-disregard" was the locus of her personal pain. It also contributed to her experiencing chronic suicidal ideation. "Deep inside," she would share with me, "I have this sense of worthlessness—that people, the world, would be better off without me." No amount of cognitive-focused logic could undo her self-torture. Years of therapy with a skilled clinician has allowed this young woman to achieve a life worth living and become the gift to our profession that the skills she displayed promised us those many years ago.

Summary

Suicide is a complexity. To understand this is to accept the individual and idiosyncratic nature of the event. Yet all too often our need is to simplify complexity. Oftentimes we want to simplify, categorize and organize so that we feel more comfortable. We struggle with ambiguities and shades of gray. Edwin Shneidman cautioned us in 1985 when he said of suicide: "Suicide is the result of an untimely convergence of multiple psychiatric, psychological, social, relational, environmental, occupational, cultural, medical, academic stressors that severely challenges an individual's capacity to cope."

We have just discussed the risk factors to suicide that are also called, depending on the source, "predisposing factors" (Jacobs and Brown, 1989) or "distal warning signs" (Moscicki,1999). These are conditions that create in an individual a vulnerability to consider suicide or other self-harm behaviors as a management or coping strategy. There are conditions that when observed in our clients should trigger further inquiry on the subject of suicide or self-harm. These issues are the focus of early intervention.

But we want to stress that although acts of suicide are idiosyncratic, there are commonalities to most, if not all, suicide events. We have gained an understanding of these commonalities from research on suicide that spans seven decades. We know, for instance, that suicide is viewed by the person, at this time in his or her life, as the best solution to unremitting and intolerable pain. We know that most, if not all, men and women who die by suicide are feeling, at the time of their death, fatalistic despair (hopelessness) and significant self-devaluation (helplessness). We know that suicide is the direct result of this hopelessness and helplessness. We know that in the mind of the suicidal individual their problems cannot be solved and they do not have the ability to solve those problems. We know that the majority—over 90 percent—of men and women who die from suicide had demonstrated symptoms of an Axis I mental disorder prior to their death, and, of those,70 percent had a mood disorder. We know that self-medicating a mental disorder with drugs significantly complicates the pathology and greatly enhances the overall risk of self-harm and suicide.

We know that suicide rarely occurs outside the context of a social stressor. We know that those stressors are usually found to be related to issues of loss: loss of relationships (aloneness); loss of health (autonomy/independence); loss of occupation (financial stress and self-esteem issues). We know that adolescents are vulnerable to "impulsive suicides" when they live in a home where there is easy access to firearms. And, finally, we know there appears to be a psychological vulnerability to suicide in the issue of faulty or weakened coping ability. Suicide/death is viewed as the "only" option available at this time for this person. The suicide risk entails constricted coping ability and narrowing of options.

CHAPTER TWO

People Who Self-Harm

B efore we begin the discussion on people who self-harm we must revisit some of the issues we covered earlier. First, and most important, we must keep in mind that all behaviors are purposeful. There is a reason men and women self-mutilate, think about suicide, act on those thoughts, and engage in other behaviors of self-harm. Those reasons, the purpose of the behaviors, is always idiosyncratic to the individual. It is essential, therefore, that we get to know that person and place these behaviors into the context of their lives. Recall Harry Stack Sullivan's advice (1954, p.52): "Who is this person and how does he/she come to be here?" As we discover this person we endeavor to locate his or her pain. This pain could be in a past, present, or future perspective. It will be this locus of pain that will assist in isolating the reasons for the self-harm actions. Marsha Linehan (1993, p.323) in her development of dialectical behavior therapy (DBT) tells us: "Self-harm behaviors (suicide and non-lethal self-mutilation) are viewed as problem-solving behaviors that function to remediate negative emotional arousal and distress." Edwin Shneidman tells us: "Almost every case of committed suicide (or serious contemplation of it) can be understood in terms of intensely felt psychological pain, with the idea that death is the best solution to the problem of intolerable 'psychache'" (1993). This pain may be placed in the context of Axis I, Axis II, Axis III, or Axis IV disorders. The intolerable nature of the pain leads the person to see self-harm behaviors as the only way out. These individuals will present to the clinician with profound

35

issues of cognitive rigidity (Levenson, 1973; Patsiokas 1979) and significant deficits in problem-solving (Goodstein, 1982). The self-harming person is challenged in coping and, therefore, suicide and self-harming behaviors become attractive solutions.

A final guideline is provided for us by Linehan (1993, p.19): "Of critical importance is to determine whether the self-harming behavior is primarily 'respondent' behavior, 'operant' behavior, or both." Behavior is *respondent* when it is automatically elicited by a situation or a specific stimulus. Suicide responses are viewed, therefore, as escape behaviors elicited by aversive conditions or intense emotional pain. Behaviors are viewed as *operant* when they are designed to achieve consequences and function to control the environment. When suicides, suicide attempts, suicidal ideation, or self-mutilation are designed to elicit care and/or attention, to get others to take one seriously, or to get into a hospital, these behaviors are considered functionally operant. When Shneidman proposed that the purpose of suicide is to seek a solution and the goal of suicide is the cessation of pain, he was proposing a view of suicide as respondent. When he and Farberow (1986) popularized the notion of suicide being "a cry for help," they talked of self-harm behaviors as being operant.

We will now address the varied forms of self-harm behaviors; ranging from the self-mutilator to the suicide completer. In each of these populations we will stress the "operant" or "respondent" goal of the behaviors and give you the idiosyncratic profile of each population.

Self-Mutilation. My own definition of self-mutilation comes from a lecture series I give on the subject. More profound definitions exist I would guess, but this is my attempt at simplification. These are behaviors that bring varied levels of pain or harm to the body for the purposes of relief from psychological/psychiatric discomfort (respondent) and/or the achievement of an unfulfilled need (operant). One issue I want to stress, however, is the significant difference between self-mutilation and suicide. Although similar in their respondent and operant goals, their difference is profound. The difference is life and death. The difference lies in understanding the intent of the activity. The goal and intent of suicide is relief from intolerable pain by cessation of life. Self-mutilators, however, want to rid themselves from intolerable levels of pain and *continue living*. In fact, Favazza (1996, p.33) defined self-mutilation as, "the direct and deliberate destruction or alteration of body tissue 'without' conscious suicide intent." Selekman (2004, p. 46) said of self-mutilation: "It is anti-suicide; it keeps people from dying." This difference is vital as we begin our exploration of self-harm behaviors (self-mutilation and suicide).

The first attempt to classify self-mutilative behaviors was by Karl Menninger in his popular book, *Man Against Himself* (1938). It was not until 1983 that another classification was offered by Pattison and Kahan. This attempt was followed by Winchel and Stanely (1991) and, not long after, by Favazza and Rosenthal (1993). Favazza's book, *Bodies Under Siege* (1996) remains the current focus for classification of this activity. In addition to the contributions made by those researchers, I would offer my own view of this behavior and its respondent and operant goals. What I offer to you now is anecdotal and is not based on empirically-sound research. It is information about self-mutilation that I have learned from my clients and their life experiences with this behavior. It is, obviously, not designed to replace or compete with current research.

Self-Mutilation for Cohesion and Social Definition. This behavior, I have discovered, is predominant in the female population and usually begins in the pre-teen years and can remain a focus until middle age. This group currently senses in their lives real, imagined, or anticipated issues of isolation and/or aloneness. They discover through varied social networking that cutting is a method of gaining attention, developing group cohesion, and claiming a self-identity (operant). It is respondent to feelings of isolation and aloneness. Sadly, I have found that this population is often dismissed with the claim of: "They are just trying to get attention." What is ironic is that this is a correct view of this population and the exact reason we *should* pay attention to them. In school settings, they often find themselves joining sub-groups of "cutters" and often yearn to be placed in residential treatment programs for the fulfillment of their "social cohesion" needs. This group is identified by the fact that they proudly display their cuts and bandages and proudly proclaim themselves to be "cutters." Again, the respondent focus of the behavior is a sense of real or imagined aloneness and the operant focus is social cohesion, self-identity and a cry for help. It is recommended that this population be treated on an outpatient basis and avoid, if at all possible, placing them on an inpatient unit or a residential program. Placement in a residential program is often viewed as a reinforcement of their social cohesion needs and, therefore, validating the cutting behavior. This population comes to our attention quite often—especially for readers who work in schools and work with adolescents. They will be recognized by the prominent nature of their behavior. They are quite eager to display their behaviors to others to gain the attention that they need at this time in their lives. Our clinical focus for this population will be their issues of loneliness and offering them alternative methods of diminishing this pain.

Self-Mutilation to Relieve Dissociative Episodes. Many years ago I had the opportunity of meeting a young woman in her late 30s who was referred to my office by a local emergency room. She had sought services at that facility for severe bleeding from a self-inflicted slash to her wrist with a razor. The emergency room physician and social worker considered her appropriate for outpatient treatment since there did not appear to be any suicidal intent to her behavior. During her initial appointment, she described to me the circumstances that led to slashing her wrist and needing emergency services.

The incident occurred on a Friday evening after she and her work friends decided to stop off at their favorite tavern for a few drinks prior to going home for the weekend. At the bar a young man approached her and asked, very politely, if anyone was sitting in the unoccupied chair which was next to her. She indicated that the chair was as it appeared—unoccupied.

He then asked her, very politely, if he could occupy the seat and she nodded approval. That was the end of their conversation. She indicated: "He didn't say a word to me the rest of the night." The young man, however, "had on the same shaving lotion that the perp who sexually assaulted me when I was little wore during the assaults."

Many theorists (Bernstein and Putnam, 1986; Saunders and Giolas, 1991) have reminded us that maladaptive traits, dysfunctional activities, and pathological behaviors in adults can often be understood as childhood defense mechanisms that are carried into adulthood. Many of our children experience painful traumas in their early lives. These traumas can become life-threatening unless they are managed. Children will manage these traumas the best they can with childhood defense mechanisms. These defense mechanisms are very important, often essential, to enable that child to survive some horrible events in their early lives. The problem comes, however, when the child moves into adolescence and adulthood and brings these defense mechanisms with them. It is during adulthood that these defense behaviors, that were vital to the child's survival, become maladaptive, dysfunctional, and/or pathological behaviors.

When she was a little girl, this woman proceeded to tell me, she would defend herself from the trauma of sexual assault by, "pretending, while he was assaulting me, that I was somewhere else. I would fantasize about being somewhere safe and loving. And I got so good at this that I actually began to have out-of-body experiences." She began, as a childhood defense mechanism, to dissociate. During her childhood this was a vital defense for her to manage the severity of this trauma. But now she is in her 30s, and she is experiencing significant issues of posttraumatic stress with a profound comorbid condition of a dissociative disorder.

So, there she was at the bar with her friends experiencing a dissociative reaction. Her friends had never witnessed this from her and had no idea what to do. She, however, knew exactly what to do. She had one of her friends take her home and it was there she engaged in an activity she had been using for 25 years to manage her "out-of-body experiences"—she began to cut herself. She describes the physical discomfort, the sight of her blood, the sense of control, the feeling of relief as all working toward diminishing the intensity of the dissociative episode. The dissociative state was the respondent condition that provoked the eventual cutting behavior.

She had been doing this for 25 years. What got her to the emergency room that night and, eventually, to my office?

She explains: "I was so embarrassed that I had an out-of-body experience in front of my friends that I got nervous and made one of the cuts too deep. It wouldn't stop bleeding so I had to go to the ER." Up to the time she walked into the ER and, soon after into my office, she had never addressed with anyone her history of child abuse or her PTSD. Dissociative disorders are almost always going to be a comorbid condition of PTSD in men and women with histories of developmental complex trauma (Herman, Perry, and van der Kolk, 1989). The respondent issue here is the relief from the psychological discomfort of dissociative experiences. This operant issue, along with her PTSD, will often be the focus of therapy with this population (Fonagy, 1997). We will, in the clinical setting, offer her alternative methods to experience this relief which will replace self-mutilation as a management skill.

Self-Mutilation to Relieve the "Body Beautiful Curse." A few years ago I had the privilege of meeting a young woman who had just been released from prison. She was referred to my office by her parole officer for addictions counseling. Her time in prison was due to extensive charges against her for prostitution. It was discovered during a pre-sentencing evaluation that her prostitution was undertaken to pay for drugs. The parole officer, therefore, felt that it would be advisable to have her undergo addictions counseling while on parole in hopes that this would diminish her vulnerability to reengage in the prostitution. What was quite remarkable about this young lady was evident during her first session. She came into my office dressed in a very uncomplimentary, extremely oversized, wool turtleneck sweater. She was of very small stature and, to say the least, her appearance was bizarre. This rather unusual presentation was displayed during the first two sessions until I received "a gift" during the third session. It was an extremely warm, humid day and she came to her third session with the wool turtleneck sweater on and sweating profusely. This gave me the opportunity to engage with her in a conversation around the nature of her choice of clothing. It is here that we need to remember that "all behaviors are purposeful." It was during this session that this young lady began to engage in a very cautious, measured fashion around her history of child sexual abuse. The story that she revealed to me over the next few months remains one of the most tragic revelations of childhood sexual abuse that I have encountered in my 40 year career. This young lady, between the ages of eight to 13, was ritualistically sexually assaulted by three predators in her life. What made this trauma even more significantly damaging was these three predators blamed her for the assaults. They did this by making comments to her on the fact that her physical attractiveness was the reason that she was being assaulted. Many readers of this book may be familiar with the works of Joseph Sabbath. Dr. Sabbath, at a conference I attended, reminds us that perhaps the most significant damage done to the abused child is the psychological imprint that the abuse places on him or her. He says, "The most significant tragedy of child abuse goes beyond the bruises" and he further says, "The tragedy is that the abused child incorporates the identity given to them by the predator." The message that this young lady received was that her physical attractiveness was the reason that she was victimized. She explains to me that starting at the age of 11 she began to wear very uncomplimentary, oversized and bizarre clothing. She also began to totally ignore her personal hygiene. She began a process to de-sexualize herself for the purposes of safety from sexual predators. This was her operant behavior. About six months into her therapy she spontaneously revealed to me severe scars on both of her arms. As she showed me the scars, she said, "I had to do something about my body beautiful curse." Her cutting and other "de-sexualizing" behaviors were respondent to this powerful "body beautiful curse." This young lady presented an example of severe scarring by individuals who acquired through early childhood messages a sense of "body self-hatred." During our therapy relationship she produced other "distancing" behaviors. She had a very subtle, but biting, sense of humor. During our first couple of months together she would use this skill to ridicule her therapist. This was another operant behavior. The message that she was giving me during this time was: "Keep your distance." Again, the reader is advised to respect that all behaviors are purposeful. This young woman's presentation was designed, during the first year of our therapy, to keep a safe "emotional distance" from me. Her cutting was also a purposeful behavior designed to keep her safe from predatory males.

Self-Mutilation to Regulate Emotion Behaviors. Behaviors such as scarring, burning, slashing, and cutting are often utilized by men and women to regulate emotions. More often than not, these men and women lack the ability to internally monitor and control emotional experiences. Because of this deficiency in the realm of internal management they learned, usually at a very early age, that maladaptive self-harm behaviors allow them to experience this much needed sense of management. What we often find among these people is that when they do experience an intense emotion, such as anger, they experience extreme levels of this emotion and an inability to manage it. This lack of management allows this intense emotion to remain disruptive in their lives for a prolonged period of time and can therefore be quite damaging in their social, vocational, occupational, and relational endeavors. Therefore, they seek to "manage" these emotions, albeit in maladaptive fashion, not solely because of their painful nature, but also because of the damage they do in the individual's life.

I remember, for example, a young man I met a number of years ago in a local hospital's emergency room. He was in his mid-20s and he was brought into the emergency room by his girlfriend after he had slashed himself quite viciously with a broken beer bottle. The doctors in the emergency room were going to admit him to a medical unit but wanted an evaluation to determine if he was appropriate and safe for placement in that environment.

During my conversation with this young man he appeared to be very calm and oriented, and he showed no signs of psychotic stimulation. After I had introduced myself and explained to him why I was there, I asked him to recount for me the incident that led him to the emergency room. He explained to me that earlier that afternoon he and his girlfriend were having an argument and he was "getting angry." He went on to explain to me his experience of anger, and it was quite obvious that he had had a lifelong history of maladaptive emotional regulation skills. For instance, he told me about an incident in his life as a 10-year-old boy when a pet cat that he had did something against his wishes. He reports that he became very angry at the cat and wanted to kill it. He then said to me that he really was ambivalent about this wish to kill his cat and in order to regulate his anger and "calm down" he took his father's cigarette lighter and burned his arm. This incident is an example of how burning, slashing, and cutting act as emotional regulators to calm patients down. He then went on to explain to me the incident of that afternoon. Because he was feeling intense anger towards his girlfriend he was feeling the urge to assault her. He reported to me, however, that he loved her very much and he did not want to hurt her. So, instead, he took a beer bottle that was on a table next to him, broke it, and began to slash himself in the chest area. He reported to me that this activity had the same calming effect as burning himself with his father's cigarette lighter had on him as a 10-year-old. He slashed himself in order to keep from hurting his girlfriend. He burned himself in order to keep from hurting his pet cat. This young man presents an excellent example of people who engage in what we term "maladaptive behaviors" in order to manage painful, disruptive emotional experiences. His cutting was a respondent behavior to his unregulated rage. From the aspect of operant goals, the cutting was used to achieve control, maintain calm, and to keep from hitting his girlfriend.

While we have spent some time here talking about the emotion of anger, we obviously need to respect that other emotions may challenge an individual person's capacity to cope and, therefore, become disruptive in their lives. These emotions could be jealousy, sadness, anxiety, depression, and so forth. I have found in my work with men or women with addiction disorders that they are vulnerable to using drugs for the purpose of regulating painful emotions. Many of the men and women that I have had the privilege of seeing over the years have used alcohol, for instance, to regulate the painful emotions of depression, sadness, and anger. I have found over the years that many men and women addicted to cannabis will use that drug to manage unregulated emotions of anxiety. Again, we are reminded that all behaviors are purposeful.

Marsha Linehan (1993) has reminded us that men and women with traits of the borderline personality disorder will have significant challenges in regulating emotions. She talks extensively about their vulnerability to cutting for management purposes. She also discusses with us that many of these men and women find that being placed in an inpatient psychiatric hospital can act as an "emotional regulator." They are, therefore, vulnerable to being multiple users of this service. We will talk in a later chapter about treatment for this population which will incorporate many of Marsha Linehan's theories.

One final word needs to be addressed regarding this population. We find that quite a few men and women who use cutting, slashing, burning for the purpose of emotional regulation have a vulnerability to becoming addicted to this behavior. Quite often, they will cut in a very painful fashion. As a matter of fact, pain is the goal of their activity. Because of this, certain chemicals are released when this pain is felt. And this chemical reaction can, in many of our clients, create a sensation that could become enjoyable and therefore addictive. As an example, I return to the gentleman in the emergency room. During my conversation with him, he actually stated: "I kind of like the calmness it gives, it chills me out, and I'm quite addicted to it." This is an aspect of these behaviors that we need to respect and explore during our treatment.

Self-Mutilation and the Emotionally-Constricted. Many people have significant difficulties in accessing emotions. This challenge may stem from a variety of different issues. Some of the men and women that we meet are challenged in accessing emotions due to the fact that as children they lived in environments that were "emotionally invalidating." These "emotionally invalidating" environments failed to give children a feeling of safety when expressing emotions. Therefore, these children had to develop other methods to convey and demonstrate their feelings. Some of these children, primarily during adolescence, discover that when they cut, it "helps me feel something." They may also discover, again during adolescence, that when they are under the influence of drugs emotions are more accessible. I have heard many people say to me, "when I cut, it helps me feel something on the outside that I otherwise only feel on the inside." The respondent behavior is the pain of being emotionally constricted. The operant issue at play here is the actualizing of the emotions through the act of cutting or burning.

I remember many years ago meeting a young woman who was 17 years old when she entered therapy with me. She was referred to me by her mother after she was found cutting herself on the wrists with a razor in her closet. It was only after a couple of sessions with this client that I got the big picture of this client's cutting episode. She explained to me during therapy that her parents had "the marriage from hell." She describes, in graphic detail, her parents' fistfights, throwing pots and pans at each other, rolling on the floor and biting each other. She then tells me about her emotional reaction to these parental battles. She became visibly agitated in my office as she attempted to describe these emotions. Finally, she just blurted out, "I get so frustrated that I go up to my room and cut myself." She then described the emotional "relief" she gained after each cutting episode. She made it very clear to me that she only cuts when her parents fight. She went to great lengths to distance herself from some of her acquaintances in school who are "cutters." For instance, she said to me "I am not an emo." I am sure those of you who work with adolescents are quite familiar with this term "emo." It is a term used primarily in middle school and high school to describe kids who are highly emotional and also, kids who cut. (See section above on self-mutilation for social cohesion.) My therapeutic goal for this patient, as with all men and women who experience emotional constriction, is to provide her with an emotionally validating therapy environment. The focus of therapy for this population is, essentially, to provide them with alternative ways to access and express emotions that will hopefully replace the maladaptive method of cutting.

Self-Mutilation and Psychosis. Perhaps the most devastating of all of the medical mental disorders is the diagnosis schizophrenia, paranoid subtype. Men and women with this diagnosis are extremely vulnerable to violent forms of self-mutilation when they are experiencing what is termed, "command, persecutory hallucinations." These hallucinations, primarily auditory, will demand them to perform a violent act towards self, and sometimes, towards others. It is a rule of thumb when working with men and women who experience psychotic behaviors to be attentive to a phenomenon called "responding to internal stimuli." During this time the client will appear distracted, oftentimes laughing or mumbling to themselves. It is essential when we observe this behavior that we ask the client if they are hearing voices. If the client responds affirmatively to that question we then ask them, "what are the voices saying to you?" If the client responds to that question with any comment that leads us to believe that these voices are command and/or persecutory in nature then immediate inpatient services should be pursued. As an example, many years ago I had an experience with a client who was responding to internal stimuli and, therefore, I pursued those questions. He responded affirmatively that he was hearing voices and then told me the voices were saying to him, "my eye is evil, I shall pluck it out." He was immediately hospitalized due to that response, for his safety and a reevaluation of his medication.

Suicide. The definition of suicide has captured the interest and fascination of theorists and scientists for generations. A very simplistic approach could be used on this topic, such as changing the definition of suicide to be self-murder. But an examination of this tragic phenomenon reveals that suicide is much more than this simplistic explanation.

There are a number of key issues that must be respected while developing an appropriate definition for suicide. One of those issues is captured in the word *intent*. If suicide is defined merely from a behavioral perspective it could result in an incomplete understanding and even a significant misunderstanding of this behavior. For instance, let me share with you some cases that I have been involved in over the years that were initially misunderstood as suicides. There was, as an example, a 34-year-old young man who died of a cocaine overdose, and the mid-40s gentleman who jumped out the window of his seventh floor apartment. And then we have the case of a 21-year-old who drove his car off the road at a high rate of speed, crashed into a tree, and died on impact. These cases, and many others, were not seen as suicides. A simple behavioral observation, however, would certainly indicate otherwise. But the key in recognizing that these behaviors were not suicidal was the issue of the decedents' *intent* at the time of their deaths. What was the intent of the 34-year-old as he ingested a lethal amount of cocaine into his body? What was the intent of the gentleman who jumped from his seventh floor apartment? What was the intent of the 21-year-old as he drove his car off the road and died as a result of its impact with a tree?

The key issue in the appropriate definition of suicide is a respect for, and a recognition of, the fact that *you cannot have a suicide without an intent to die.* This may appear to be very basic, but it is of core importance when an individual explores the issue of suicide. It was recognized that the 34-year-old who died of an overdose of cocaine died accidentally. His capacity for rational thought was so significantly impaired by his bingeing on cocaine that he miscalculated the lethality of his usage. The gentleman who jumped from his seventh floor apartment was also seen as death by accident due to the fact that prior to his death he had a delusion that he was Superman. His friends were ridiculing him for this delusion, so he decided to prove to his friends that he was indeed Superman by jumping out the window, fully believing that he was going to be able to fly like Superman. And, finally, the 21-year-old was severely intoxicated at the time of his death, lost control of his car and died by accident.

Another key issue in the definition of suicide is the cognitive awareness that the activity one is engaging in has the potential to end one's existence. This issue is a key concern when we discuss later on the issue of lethality. Throughout all of these conversations on the definition of suicide there remains one constant element. That element is: Suicide is a complexity. It is not, therefore, easily defined or understood. All too often in our haste to understand this tragic issue in our society we offer up simplistic explanations for why a person would take his or her own life. This need to simplify the complex nature of suicide can result in some unfortunate misunderstandings and thus to significant misdirection in treating the suicidal person. For instance, there is a tragic misunderstanding of the role of depression in relation to suicide. Depression is a primary correlate to completed suicide, but there is, unfortunately, a belief that depression causes suicide. Depression is the major correlate to suicide in men, whereas, in females, the issue most powerfully correlated to suicide is depression with post-partum onset. Suicide is not caused by any singular issue in a person's life. Instead, suicide is the tragic result of a complexity of issues that are literally bombarding a person. The reason this misunderstanding is of such a great concern is it could lead to the belief that if we can effectively identify and treat the depressed person we will eliminate the scourge of suicide in our society. While it is obviously of great importance to diagnose and treat depression, that alone may not prevent a person from considering suicide. As mentioned earlier, approximately 70 percent of men and women who died by suicide, and who were eventually studied, were suffering from depression at the time of their deaths. Depression, however, is a very common malady among our citizens. An estimated 20 million men and women in the United States are treated for this medical mental disorder in any given year. The overwhelming majority of those people do NOT die by suicide. Only a very small percentage of men and women with depression die by suicide. But when a suicide does occur, depression is the primary correlate. Therefore, the question raised is: Why them? What made that person, whose depression increased their vulnerability to suicide, eventually take his or her life? That will be the focus of the next section.

The Suicide Ideator. Suicidal ideation is a period of time (with the time span identified by the person) where levels of stress become so unbearable they defy that person's coping capacity. Suicide thoughts, therefore, are entertained as coping strategies and problem solvers—a method to eliminate unbearable levels of psychological pain. These unbearable levels of pain are individually defined. Edwin Shneidman (1985, p. 74) said it best when he claimed: "One person's unbearable pain could be another person's irksome event." It is vital for all of us to respect that our clients retain the right to define where they hurt. They will define their pain to us in the context of their lives and world view. We *do not* agree or disagree with our clients' definition of where they hurt—we accept it. Shneidman goes on to urge us (p. 38): "The first task of therapy is to go to the locus of the client's pain." There are multiple frames and shapes that this pain takes. The most common form—to a point where causality could possibly be established—is the mental anguish of anxiety, depression, or psychosis. The stimulus for this pain is often *loss*. We discussed these issues of loss in our previous chapter when we discussed losses correlated to suicide as risk factors. The ideator sees death as the end of this pain, often looking forward to "nothingness" as the elimination of these unbearable torments. The ideator, also, often thinks of death as a "rebirth." The pain is gone, finished forever. But they are, often, reborn into a new life. This latter concept is the one most often entertained by children and adolescents.

Let's explore this population and emphasize a number of markers that are important to understand. First of all, suicidal ideation is very common. David Clark, an epidemiologist with Rush Research Center in Chicago, noted years ago: "thinking about suicide is very common; dying from it is quite rare" (1992, p.201). Research, in a number of settings, reveals that millions of people think about suicide in any given year. Think for just a brief minute of the unimaginable nightmare of your life: What is the worst possible thing that could happen to you? Imagine the emotional pain that you would experience. Imagine how it would exceed your current capacity to cope. Imagine how you might entertain wishes for death to eliminate this pain. For the ideator, suicide is seen, at this moment of their lives, as very reasonable; a useful problem-solving strategy. For this reason we are reminded never to pathologize suicidal ideation or the suicide ideator. In fact, we must be empathic to a point of normalizing it. We offer you the example of the 58-year-old woman who suddenly loses her husband to a heart attack. He is walking out of church on a beautiful Sunday morning, collapses and dies. He dies one month before his retirement, an event he and his wife had been eagerly anticipating. He is a wonderful husband, father, friend, and person. His wife is devastated in her grief. She begins to cope by drinking, which provides her with transient relief. She then begins to seek permanent relief with thoughts of death. For this woman, at this time in her life, suicide is seen as the only way out of her grief. In Chapter 4 of this book, when we discuss the treatments for the self-harming and suicidal populations, we will talk about our treatment goal which is to expand coping options or, as Edwin Shneidman (1985) said: "We remove the client's blinders and offer them other ways to resolve their unbearable pain." But at this point in time the intense grief is unbearable. It defies her current capacity to cope. Suicide becomes her ultimate problem-solving strategy.

Another feature that we must explore about this population of suicide ideators is that all are vulnerable. Suicide ideation has no respect for age, gender, race, culture, educational status, religious affiliation, or socioeconomic status. Anybody, under the right circumstances, can become a suicide ideator. The wonderful aspect of this population, however, is that they are ambivalent about their suicidal thoughts. This ambivalence stems from many factors. The most important is that the ideator still has hope. We have stressed in this book, and we will continue to stress, the vital importance of respecting the issue of hope and hopelessness. Again, hopelessness is the primary fueling emotion for suicide. Suicide is the direct result of despair. If an individual has a shred of hope this will greatly diminish his or her risk for completing suicide. (Again, in Chapter 4, I will further discuss the therapist's role in instilling and nurturing hope in our therapeutic alliance with our clients.) Because of this ambivalence, suicide ideators openly communicate their suicidal fears. They will eagerly discuss with you where they hurt or the locus of their pain. They will discuss with you that this current pain defies their coping capacity. And they will discuss with you their wish to die. Men and women who are experiencing suicidal ideation are very open to counseling. In fact, they are very motivated during counseling. They will point out to you in full detail the locus of their pain and they will be very open to your empathic response. Your work is to offer them alternatives to suicide to resolve that pain. Overall, this population has an excellent prognosis. There really should never be any reason for these individuals to become "suicide completers." However, research has shown that ideators move into the realm of completers after a disruption in the therapeutic alliance, as defined by the client. It could be something as simple as the therapist's lack of empathy to the client's pain. Or it could be the therapist acting out of inappropriate fear, anxiety, or caution and hospitalizing the client. In Chapter 3 of this book, we will discuss those markers that the therapist needs to be aware of that may indicate a need for inpatient safety. We will also discuss some of the idiosyncratically defined disruptions in the therapy alliance that could lead a client to hopelessness. In our earlier discussion of self-harm and suicide as being respondent or operant, we would view the suicidal ideator as both. Their suicidal wishes and thoughts are respondent to their unbearable levels of pain, and they are also operant as in verbalizing their intent: They verbalize the wish to be attended.

The Suicide Attempter. This term is widely misunderstood and misused in mental health service systems. Part of what we want to accomplish here is to clarify exactly what a suicide attempt is and what it is not. We also want to comment on some activities that are often confused with this act. Suicide attempters are people with an *intent* to die. Their goal is death. It is this intent that will distinguish the attempt and the ideation. The critical issue here, however, is that a history of suicide attempts is a powerful correlate to eventual death by suicide. Any client with a history of suicide attempts should be taken very seriously and attended with caution. Who exactly is the "suicide attempter"? Let us examine this behavior and describe this population.

A suicide attempter is an individual who has committed a potentially lethal act where the intent was to die. The activity was, however, reversible (cutting, slashing, overdosing, gassing) and the attempter was accidentally rescued, against his or her wishes, with the result that they survive. As an example: A young man, severely depressed over his inability to overcome a serious drug dependency issue, decides to take his life. His mother leaves for work each morning at 6 AM and does not return until 4 PM. One morning he gives his mother a half hour to get to work, runs a hot bath (he has read that hot water stimulates bleeding), takes a razor to both of his arms, and begins to bleed. His mother, on her way to work, realizes she has forgotten the keys to her building and turns her car around. Since the young man's car was still in the driveway she comes in the house, calls his name and gets no response. She walks up stairs, sees her son in the bathtub, calls the local emergency response, and saves his life. That is a suicide attempt. The issue is that if the mother had not forgotten her work keys this young man would have died. The circumstances of rescue lead us to the conclusion that his rescue was accidental and against his wishes. As we will stress in our next chapter, we must capture this intent in our clients since this history is a powerful correlate to eventual death by suicide. It may also show us a focal point of the client's pain and thus, perhaps, the central focus of therapy.

We used the term reversible activity in our previous description of the attempter. A reversible suicide activity is an act where, from the beginning of the activity to the moment it leads to death, there is a brief window of time for rescue. Cutting, slashing, overdosing, gassing are common reversible activities. From the moment a person takes the razor to the skin there is an opportunity for rescue before that act causes death. Sometimes that activity is accidentally interrupted and, at other times, it is self-interrupted. I remember hearing one of the rare survivors of a leap off the Golden Gate Bridge claim, "as soon as my hand left the rail, I knew I had made a mistake." That is a sobering comment. Many of you may have seen data on attempters vs. completers. If you have, you will have noticed that the majority of *attempters* are female while the majority of *completers* are male. One reason for this divergence is that the female will more often use reversible methods, while the male, more often than not, will employ irreversible methods such as shooting or hanging— methods where there is NO window for rescue. Therefore, in another category of suicide attempters is the person who has committed a potentially lethal act where the intent is to die, but it is reversible, and they panic and self-interrupt. In this panic state, they very often seek rescue, and they often need immediate medical attention or they will die. That is a suicide attempt. The key issue in this population will be the state of panic. They will often beg, during rescue, "don't let me die." An example is a young woman, recently rejected in an intimate relationship. She impulsively takes a razor to her arms and begins to bleed. She panics, calls for rescue, is taken to a local emergency room where she needs immediate medical attention or she will die from loss of blood. She claims to the ER staff: "I wanted to die, but when I saw all the blood I went into a panic." This panic state has received quite a bit of attention from studies. It appears to be the result of the sudden, jolting awareness of impending death. It is ironic that when studying suicide one is confronted with so many incongruent features. One minute the person is yearning for death as a way out of unbearable pain, and then, when confronted with the reality of death, there is that life-saving panic…the need to survive.

The final category of suicide attempters are the folks who have a degree of certainty, often wrongly assessed, that a specific activity will terminate their existence. The activity fails to achieve that goal and they are significantly upset at this failure. They will often claim afterwards: "I can't even kill myself the right way." An example would be an adolescent, recently rejected in a meaningful relationship, who responds by swallowing a handful of a parent's antidepressant medication and lying down waiting to die. Seven hours later he is still alive and very upset. Such attempters will often tell the parent what they did. The key is that for that brief moment they had an intent to die and they are very angry that they did not succeed. Depending on how this act is addressed by the individual or the social support system this individual may continue to entertain thoughts of suicide and revisit a life threatening activity at a later date.

While these three activities are usually seen as the common focus for describing suicide attempts, we must differentiate them from other behaviors often mistakenly termed "attempts." These behaviors range from non-lethal self-mutilation behaviors to suicide gesturing to calculated self-harm activity for secondary gain. An examination of these behaviors is important as it helps us describe with clarity behaviors that are, indeed, suicide attempts.

Self-mutilation, which has been described earlier in this chapter, is differentiated from suicide attempts by intent. The intent of suicide is to terminate existence and end pain. The intent of self-mutilation is to continue to live and to "manage" pain. In fact, self-mutilation is often called "anti-suicide" behavior as it actually keeps a person from thinking about or attempting suicide. In no way is this designed to reduce our concern over the issue of self-mutilation. We, obviously, remain alert to this group. We are, however, cautious in calling them "suicidal." Again, the issue of intent is of utmost importance. The young woman who cuts her wrist so she can manage her vulnerability to dissociate can hardly be called suicidal since her intent for the act of cutting is distinctly different from the young man who slashes his wrist in order to bleed to death. The treatment for both populations has similarities, but the caution of using inpatient safety with the suicide attempter is going to be much more important than seeking a similar setting for the non-suicidal self-mutilator.

Alan L. Berman discussed, at a conference I attended many years ago, the concept of "behavioral rehearsal" for suicide. He talked about his familiarity with people who died by suicide and, prior to their death, practiced the activity that was eventually used to take their lives. He remarked on the individual who died by hanging and, prior to his death, was found tying a rope or tightening a belt around his neck. He assumed that this person, and many like him, was rehearsing the suicide act. The goal, he assumed, was to become familiar with the activity, to get used to it for the purpose of decreasing the anxiety connected with ending one's life. These folks are commonly referred to as "suicide gesturers." They are planning suicide with these activities and should be taken very seriously. They are not, however, suicide attempters. At the time of their activity they are not intending to die; the goal is to practice the activity to decrease the associated anxiety. It is important to understand the hierarchy from the self-mutilator who is cutting in a calculated fashion in order to get relief from anxiety, to the suicide gesturer who is cutting to get familiar with how the razor feels against the skin, as opposed to the person who is cutting for the purpose of exsanguination and eventual death—the suicide attempter/completer.

Finally, it is important to discuss men and women who use suicidal threats and/or calculated self-harm activities for secondary gain. As we revisit our consideration of respondent and operant conditions that motivate behaviors, we discover in these folks some fascinating dynamics. It is well documented in the work of Linehan (1993) that men and women with features of the borderline personality have significant difficulty in dealing with stress, regulating emotions, and tolerating rejection and abandonment in relationships. These respondent conditions may motivate them to use threats of suicide or calculated self-harm activities to gain access to settings (in-patient psychiatric facilities) that may help them achieve management over these challenging events (operant conditions). These people are not acutely suicidal, but they present as such (and sometimes do so chronically) to gain help with their issues. These presentations come in different shapes and sizes. They are, however, recognized by the feature of secondary gain. Examples are numerous: "If you don't put me in the hospital, I'm going to kill myself;" "if you leave me, I'm going to kill myself;" "if you fire me, I'm going to kill myself." And they present with varied levels of risk—the homeless individual who presents in a hospital's emergency room threatening suicide on a sub-freezing night to gain access to shelter for the night, the individual recently charged with a crime who uses suicide threats to gain access to a psychiatric facility for the purpose of assisting in his legal defense, the young man who threatens to kill himself if his current girlfriend leaves him as she has just threatened, the young woman severely lacking in emotional regulation skills and stress tolerance skills who, in a frenzied state, seeks hospitalization to soothe her emotional upheaval. We treat all of these folks with respect and dignity. And, also, as we will discuss in our final chapter, we treat them.

In the next chapter, we are going to discuss how to assess your clients for a history of suicide attempts. I am going to offer a user-friendly protocol designed to discover if your current client has a positive history for a suicide attempt. This is of vital importance. On average, over their lifetimes about 10-15 percent of individuals making suicide attempts eventually go on to kill themselves (Roy and Linnoila, 1990). A history of suicide attempts is considered a primary risk factor and correlates to eventual death by suicide. It is strongly recommended that all therapists routinely screen new clients and/or patients for a history of suicide activity.

The Suicide Completer. This is the term used to describe men and women who die by suicide. They pursue an activity that they know, if allowed to go unattended, will kill them. Death is the ultimate intent of this activity. These types of activities are fueled by the two vital emotions for suicide: hopelessness and helplessness. Ronald Maris (1992), speaks of this hopelessness when he discusses the "process of suicide." He states:

> One key to predicting suicide is that lifelong repetition of similar problems breaches an adaptive threshold in some individuals but not in others (and we need to know why this happens). Apparently, almost anyone can (and routinely does) weather single, acute crisis. Suicidal hopelessness is made up of very different stuff: repeated loss, repeated depression, repeated hospitalization, chronic aloneness, chronic physical and/or emotional pain, progressive loss of social support, repeated failures, and the like.

This issue of hopelessness is the primary feature in the identification of the high-risk suicide completer. The helplessness of the completer is evidenced by weakened self-validation. They do not see themselves as capable of solving life's problems. This penetrating awareness creates a lethal element of self-directed rage and devaluation.

The profile of the suicide completer contains elements that all clinicians must be aware of. They include the following: being male, white, and 25 years of age or older; being separated, widowed, or divorced; living alone and/or having no sense of social cohesion; being unemployed or retired; being in poor physical health; having a medical mental disorder of mood, anxiety and/or psychosis; drug dependency (predominantly alcohol dependency); having visited a primary care physician within six months of the suicide (or attempt); having a history positive for suicide attempts where firearms, hanging, or jumping was the method and the individual was immediately rescued by accidental discovery and against their wishes; not reporting suicidal intent to others; and leaving a suicide note. Eventual suicide is particularly likely when there is significant social isolation, when there are significant elements of a mental disorder, and when substance use is designed to manage and/or control the symptoms of the mental disorder (co-occurring disorders or the self-medicating mentally ill). Verbalized metaphors of hopelessness and helplessness are also seen as significant correlates to completed suicide. The most concerning element in this profile is the lack of communication about the suicidal intent. Allow me to operationalize some of these elements with cases showing how these issues may be displayed by clients.

A 44-year-old white male is ordered into treatment by the local drug court diversion program. The initial mental status exam conducted during intake revealed some diagnostic and treatment concerns. He appeared for his intake session in a timely fashion. Dress and grooming were of concern as he was wearing a thin coat when temperatures were below freezing. His clothes were ragged and torn. Personal hygiene was of concern as he had a distinct body odor and was poorly groomed. His attitude was passive with an economy of speech and responses. He established poor eye contact, and his affect was subdued with a dysphoric mood. He appeared much older than his stated age and had a continuous, productive cough. His fingers were nicotine stained, and he asked repeatedly if he could smoke during our session. He was visibly agitated and upset when I denied him that request. He indicated that his sleep, appetite, and energy level were poor. He was currently homeless and indicated that, with few exceptions, this has been his state for over 20 years. His only source of pleasure was smoking crack. He indicated that he started using cocaine while in college and had been using on a continuous basis also for over 20 years. He was oriented to time, place, person, and reason for interview. He did not display any bizarre or delusional thoughts. When he did engage in conversation he showed a high level of intelligence. He left college after his second year of "courses in pre-law." He refused to elaborate on the circumstances of his terminating his education.

He made it very clear during the interview that he was not with me of his own volition. He was "coerced" by the court. His use of projection, blame, denial of personal responsibility, and rationalizing behaviors were pronounced defense mechanisms. He indicated that he had no intention of stopping drug use and said: "Telling me to quit my cocaine is like telling me to stop breathing." He was reluctant to discuss childhood issues other than to say he was "estranged from my parents at a very early age." When asked to elaborate, he refused by telling me: "That's none of your business." He stated that he was married and divorced twice and had four children; two from each marriage. He, again, refused to provide further information on family or marital issues. He did, however, add that he had "not seen my kids in years...I have no idea where they are." There was a hint of sadness in this reply and when I reflected that, he became very defensive and wanted to know, "what this has to do with my drug use?" I asked him about friends and he laughed and said, "my crack buddies." He then spontaneously offered: "I don't even know their names...we just get high together" He then offered: "Really...nobody out there gives me a thought." I asked about medical care and he reported that he hasn't been seen by a medical professional in over 20 years. When asked about employment history he indicated that he has an "aimless existence." He did refer to a history of periodic part time employment in janitorial, maintenance, dishwashing jobs. They usually lasted three or four weeks. Then he would quit. He stated, "I get bored easily." I asked about other drug use and he indicated that while cocaine is predominant he also drinks. He voluntarily added, "when I'm lonely I'll go to a bar and have a few beers just to have someone to talk to. You know, people like me better when I'm drunk...I can be an entertaining guy." When asked what crack/cocaine does for him he said, "it keeps me alert...helps me stay awake." He acknowledged night-time traumas. He said he served in the military and was in Vietnam for a year. When I asked for further information on his military experience he shut me down: "That is one thing I do not talk about...so you need to get that very clear." He denied any history of treatment for substance use or mental health concerns. When I asked about a history of suicide activity he mentioned an attempt when he was younger. He elaborated by adding: "I tried to hang myself, but someone found me." He refused to talk about the circumstances of his rescue, but added, "I think about it every day." I asked him if he were to decide upon suicide as a solution whether he would share his plans with another person. His response was: "Who would I tell? Nobody gives a damn about me...even if someone did (care), I probably wouldn't say anything."

Edwin Shneidman, the icon of the study of suicide in our society, made a comment years ago that was quite chilling. "I want to tell you about a client I saw a while back who I knew was going to die by suicide and there was nothing I could do to stop him." He was roundly criticized for this comment. We never give up or lose hope with our clients. But, I believe what he was trying to impress upon us was that we do the best we can, but there are times we will not succeed in keeping our clients alive.

What are your thoughts on this client? Examine his profile. Be alert to his risk factors. At the very least we know he meets many of the criteria that are considered risks for completed suicide. What is fascinating about this young man is that in this initial session he gave me a gift—he articulated the locus of his pain. He told me where he hurt and if he was going to engage in therapy at all, this was the topic he would consider discussing.

Other Suicidal Populations to Consider

Before we conclude this chapter on suicide and self-mutilation, I want to address two other populations that may appear in your practices. Those populations are: Homicide/Suicide and Suicide/Homicide.

The Homicide/Suicide Population. This is an impulse to kill another and then the self because of a disruption in an intimate relationship in which coercive means were used to control the partner. This disruption, therefore, challenges the need to control; their possessiveness and narcissism. The primary goal of the act is to kill the partner (homicide). The suicide of the perpetrator is designed to avoid legal consequences. The realm of this tragic scene: Cluster C Personality Disorders, where the perpetrator is often demonstrating traits, if not the complete criteria, for the diagnosis of the Obsessive-Compulsive Personality Disorder and the partner carries traits, if not the complete criteria, for either the Dependent or the Avoidant Personality Disorder. The perpetrators are usually male in the age group of 16 to 55. They have a history of chronic unemployment, social isolation, and predatory behaviors. They demonstrate cognitive rigidity, extreme possessiveness in relationships, insecurity, and impulse control and emotional regulation deficits. They often are survivors of significant child psychological and physical abuse. Perpetrators of this act often affiliate themselves with social settings or organizations that reinforce their control needs in relationships. They often show up at treatment centers for couples counseling at the urging of the controlled partner. At times they will appear for counseling under coercion at the order of the legal system for substance use issues or domestic violence charges. They will never come to therapy of their own volition. They may be highly defended with demonstrable attachment pathology. They tend to be extremely resistant in therapy and have a poor prognosis. They will leave couples counseling when they fear that the counseling may interfere with their control of their social environment. They will take the partner with them and refuse to allow the partner to return to individual therapy. They will be motivated toward homicide/suicide when the partner begins to display signs and behaviors of autonomy. These autonomous behaviors may be as simple as joining a social network on the internet, joining a book club, developing a friendship with the next door neighbor. Treatment for the partner has to be very cautious and always with professional consultation. When the partner moves to complete independence/autonomy and the perpetrator feels no control is when the greatest threat will be experienced. Therapists urging these clients to autonomy may actually heighten the client's risk for harm.

The Suicide/Homicide Population. These people have the impulse to kill a loved one out of a misguided sense of altruism. The perpetrator is hopeless and helpless in relation to a sense of pain in a loved one. The suicide is the primary intent consequent to an inability to effectively intervene in a loved one's condition, and the homicide is seen as the act of altruism. There are two profiles in this population: the elderly male caring for the elderly female partner who is in significant physical and/or psychological pain due to a terminal or chronic illness and the adult female in an abusive, possessive relationship who is caring for children under 18 who are also being abused.

In both of these profiles, it is the sense of hopelessness and helplessness that fuels the suicidal intent of the perpetrator. This is then coupled with the misguided sense of altruism (they would be better off dead) that leads to the homicide. Therefore, the clinician must remain alert to the sense of hopelessness and helplessness when working with these two situations. In the female we also need to remain alert to post-partum depression with psychotic features which may compound this risk. Quite often these two profiles will self-medicate their sense of despair with drug use—primarily alcohol. They will talk about feelings of shame and isolation, remorse and guilt. Their prognosis, if they are reached early in this process, is good. They will talk about wanting to die and they will make specific suicide/homicide plans which often take the form of a "pact" with the victim(s).

As we conclude this chapter we are reminded that there is a reason why men and women self-mutilate, think about suicide and die from suicide. That reason is to either manage or eliminate unbearable levels of emotional, psychiatric, or psychological pain. We have and will continue to stress that the first task of therapy is to discover the locus and feel of that pain—the purpose for the self-mutilation and suicide.

CHAPTER THREE

Assessments

I was told years ago, by a person much wiser than I: "We treat people, not behaviors. We diagnose people, not behaviors. We assess people, not behaviors." I have taken that message to heart throughout most of my career and it has paid large dividends. That very wise person also told me that "there are three components to a good assessment: listen, listen and listen." We are reminded of the quote by Monty Roberts in his book, *The Man Who Listens to Horses:* "If you act like you have 15 minutes to hear a person's story, it will take you a lifetime to get the whole picture, but, if you act like you have a lifetime to hear a person's story you will get everything you need in 15 minutes."

Many of you are aware of the social experiment conducted a number of years ago in Washington, DC, at one of their Metro stations. On a cold January morning in 2007, a man with a violin played six Bach pieces for about an hour. During that time approximately 2000 people went through the station, most of them on their way to work. After about three minutes a middle-aged man noticed that there was a musician playing. He slowed his pace and stopped for a few seconds, and then he hurried on to meet his schedule. About four minutes later the violinist received his very first dollar. A woman threw money in a hat and, without stopping, continued to walk. About six minutes after that a young man leaned against the wall to listen to him, then looked at his watch and started to walk again. About ten minutes after that a three-year-old boy stopped, but his mother tugged him along hurriedly. The child stopped to look at the violinist again, but the mother pushed hard and the child continued to walk, turning his head the whole time. This action was repeated by several other children, but every parent, without exception, forced their children to move on quickly. About 45 minutes into his music the musician had played continuously but only six people had stopped to listen. About 20 people gave him money, but continued to walk at their normal pace. At the end of his play the man had collected a total of $32. After one hour he finished playing and silence took over. No one noticed and no one applauded. There was no recognition at all. No one knew this, but the violinist was Joshua Bell, one of the greatest musicians in the world. He played one of the most intricate pieces ever written, on a violin worth $3.5 million. Two days before, Joshua Bell had sold out a theater in Boston where the seats averaged $200-$500 apiece. The audience was entertained by the very same piece of music that he played in the Washington subway that morning. The basic message of this often told tale: Listen, listen, and listen. Listen to our clients and their stories, listen to our clients and their metaphors, listen to our clients tell us about themselves.

As we begin our conversation on assessments for suicide and other self-harming behaviors I would like to offer for the reader a very brief review of some current suicide and self- harm behaviors prediction scales. The reasoning behind this review is to assist the reader in determining the value of individual suicide prediction scales. We need to be respectful of the fact that many of these scales are useful for specific populations under specific circumstances. If we, for instance, use an individual scale that was designed for the assessment of inpatient psychiatric clients on a group of outpatient substance abuse clients we could be in grave error. We also need to respect that many of these scales are not culturally competent, meaning that their validity was assessed on a sample group of Caucasian males. And finally, we need to be aware that many of the scales I am going to be addressing with you have varied benefits in assessing suicide and self-harm risk.

What, exactly, we are assessing? We have been told over the years that the prediction of suicide is extremely difficult, if not impossible. Motto, Heilbron and Juster (1985) urged us to respect the use of and limitations of suicide assessment and or prediction scales.

> Suicide prediction scales are explicit psychological test instruments that are designed to standardize information transfer from the potentially suicidal person to the clinician. Because of the low frequency of suicide and the dire consequences of an error in the judgment that a person is not suicidal, the development and evaluation of subscales are not to be seen as standard psychometric exercises. Indeed, even the possibility of prediction of this form of violent behavior continues to be debated. However, my approach is that of focusing on the prediction of risk of the behavior rather than prediction of the behavior itself. That, I feel, would justify the continuing use and interest in the area of standardized suicide prediction scales. These evaluations, assessments, and prediction scales will focus on information that the clinician needs to make decisions about the probable future actions of the distressed patient.

Now I would like to review, very briefly, some current suicide prediction scales and talk about their peculiarities and their applications.

I would like to begin this review with a discussion of the work done by a James Eyman and Suzanne Eyman (1992) on the value of using the Rorschach, the Thematic Apperception Test (TAT), and the Minnesota Multiphasic Personality Inventory (MMPI) in the assessment of suicidality. These authors emphasize that the one positive of these measurements is the information it can deliver on the "process" of suicidality. However, research done by Eyman and Eyman suggested that the use of the Rorschach, the TAT, and the MMPI give the clinician very little accurate information on the issue of potential suicide or self-harm behaviors. The most effective way to ascertain whether a person is contemplating suicide or other self-harm behaviors is to interview that person.

Eyman and Eyman did find, however, that the Rorschach can be useful in assessing suicide risk if it is used with appropriate clinical judgment. The problem with that, however, is that this could be said of just about any other measurement available today. With the TAT, the reviewers discovered very little utility in assessing suicide or self-harm potential. And, finally, with the MMPI they found that suicidal ideation was powerfully correlated with an elevation in the depression and masculinity-femininity scales. They also discovered that a peak on the depression scale was particularly characteristic of male patients who attempt suicide by hanging. The Eymans' findings regarding the use of the MMPI in suicide evaluations for the adolescent population were interesting. They found that elevated MMPI scale scores for hypochondriasis and masculinity-femininity were significantly higher for those adolescent boys who attempted suicide than for the adolescent male non-attempters. Suicidal adolescent girls who attempted suicide had significantly higher scale scores on the depression and hysteria scales than did adolescent female non-attempters. Unfortunately, despite considerable research effort, no MMPI item, scale, or profile configuration has been found to differentiate consistently between suicidal and non-suicidal individuals. The MMPI, therefore, cannot be recommended as a tool for assessing suicide risk. At the time of this research there had been no evaluation of the benefits of the MMPI-2, but there were hopes that this vehicle may provide more valid indicators of suicidality.

While the Rorschach, TAT, and MMPI are not particularly useful instruments for the assessment of acute, immediate suicide risk, many components of these measurements are important in determining the pervasiveness of suicidal ideation and some aspects of intent such as specific plans. It was recommended by Eyman and Eyman that in assessing suicide vulnerability it would be important to use a battery of psychological tests and avoid reliance on only one instrument. For instance, they claim, that the Rorschach and TAT will supply different types of psychological information that would be useful even though some of that information does overlap considerably. In the end, their concern was to avoid using just one measurement to determine at-risk suicidal or self-harming clients. They recommended that, in order to gain a fuller and more enriched view of a person's psychological functioning, a battery of psychological tests and measurements should be utilized.

As we begin our review of other suicide prediction scales we need to clarify certain terminology that will be used. One term is *sensitivity*. Sensitivity is defined to mean the fraction of the total examined who commit suicide during a designated follow-up, and whom the scale correctly scored as being high at-risk. In other words, tests with high sensitivity are less apt to result in false negatives. And then we have the term, *specificity*, which refers to the fraction of those people evaluated who do not commit suicide and for whom the scale has correctly scored as being at low risk. High specificity results in fewer false positives. I also want to differentiate between the two groups of scales that we are going to review. One group of scales will be those that relied on the subject (the patient) as the informant. The other group will be those that relied on a second party as an informant. We begin by talking about those scales that relied on the subject as the informant.

Subject Self-Informant Scales

The Hopelessness Scale *(Beck, Weissman, Lester, and Trexler, 1974)* A self-reporting set of true-false statements. While the sensitivity for this scale was acceptable for both inpatient and outpatient adults, its weakness appears to be the subjectivity of the self-reported responses resulting in many of the responses being "socially desirable responses." The sensitivity was lower when the measurement was applied to the adolescent population.

The Index of Potential Suicide *(Zung, 1974)* This scale was intended for adults with suicide ideation. It showed very poor predictive power *(Petrie and Chamberlain, 1985)* and was unrelated to present suicidal ideation as well as future ideation suicide attempts.

The Reasons for Living Inventory *(Linehan, Goodstein, Nielson, and Chiles, 1983)* This instrument consists of 48 true/false self-report questions applying to college students and senior citizens. Sensitivity and specificity studies indicate that this can be a valuable tool, along with the clinical interview, to assess suicide ideation and intent.

The Suicide Probability Scale *(Cull and Gill, 1982)* In over 1000 Veterans Administration patients this scale scored high for sensitivity and low for specificity. Other evaluations found it weak in its inability to identify suicidal intent.

The Suicide Risk Measure *(Plutchik, Van Praag Conte, and Picard, 1999)* This is a yes-no self-report measure for use with college students and inpatient psychiatric populations. It was found helpful in identifying potential suicide attempters. Specificity and sensitivity scales were moderate.

Second-Party Informant Scales

The Clinical Instrument to Estimate Suicide Risk (CIESR) *(Motto, Heilbron, and Juster 1985)* This instrument was developed for adults hospitalized for depression. Lettieri (1974) found predictive validity in a 2-year follow-up study. A subsequent study by Clark, Young, Scheftner, Fawcett, and Fogg (1987) was unable to replicate Lettieri's findings, though they did not definitely invalidate them.

The Instrument for the Evaluation of Suicide Potential (IESP) *(Cohen, Motto, and Seiden, 1986)* This instrument is used to predict suicide among hospitalized attempters. It has low sensitivity and high specificity results.

The Intent Scale *(Pierce, 1981)* This scale was designed to determine suicide intent in inpatients who deliberately self-injure. In 1981, Pierce completed his own five-year follow-up study noting "good predictive validity."

The Los Angeles Suicide Prevention Center Scale This scale is based on hotline data collected from telephone counselors. It later became the source of the **Suicidal Death Prediction Scale** *(Lettieri, p.58)*. A drawback is the subjective interpretation of risk by the telephone counselors, many of whom were not mental health professionals.

The Neuropsychiatric Hospital Suicide Prediction Schedule *(Farberow and MacKinnon, 1975)* The focus of this instrument was on hospitalized suicide attempters. It was designed to predict future suicidal behaviors. Scoring was done by staff members based on behaviors and "emotional status." The scale correctly identified 79 percent of attempters who later died by suicide, but misidentified 25 percent who did not die by suicide.

The Scale for Assessing Suicide Risk *(Tuckman and Youngman, 1988)* This scale was derived from police reports of attempters who eventually died by suicide. It is based on the subjective judgment of the interviewer.

The Suicide Death Prediction Scale *(1974)* This scale was based on demographic variables derived from the hospital records of suicidal patients who later died from suicide. Currently used exclusively by suicide hotlines and help lines to determine callers at risk for completed suicide.

The Short Risk Scale (SRS) *(Pallis, Gibbons, and Pierce, 1984)* Its specificity and sensitivity were excellent. The focus is predicting future suicide completions from suicide attempts.

The Suicide Intent Scale *(Beck, Schuyler, and Herman, 1974)* Its focus was to determine intent of suicide attempters and to determine if they were completers based on a review of the circumstances of the rescue and the attempt behavior.

SAD PERSONS *(Patterson, Dohn, Bird, and Patterson, 1983)* This instrument was developed to help medical students determine which psychiatric patients could benefit from inpatient admission due to high levels of suicide risk. Its perspective and interpretation are very subjective.

The Suicide Potential Scale (SPS) *(Dean, Miskimins, DeCook, Wilson, and Maley, 1997)* This scale was developed for adults in hospitals and crisis centers, and is based on the subjective judgment of the interviewer. A predictive validity of 58 percent was found during an eight-year follow-up study.

The Scale for Predicting Subsequent Suicidal Behavior (SPSSB) *(Buglas and Horton, 1974)* This scale was developed from patients admitted to a poison treatment center. It had moderate to poor specificity and sensitivity ratings in a number of outcome studies.

I would like to finish this brief exploration of suicide prediction scales with some comments on these measurements. Using any psychometric evaluation or assessment scale to determine suicide potential has limited benefits. The clinician is strongly encouraged never to rely on the application of a single measurement scale to validate or invalidate suicide risk. To do so can have dire effects on treatment outcomes and could be a disaster during any possible litigation. Instead, it is recommended that psychometric measurements be used to support clinical judgment. Again, *assess the person and not the behaviors*.

That being said, I would like to offer three assessment formats used to determine risk in certain areas: 1) assessing when to hospitalize the suicide ideator; 2) assessing at intake whether the client has a history of suicide attempts; 3) assessing the intent and lethality of the suicide attempter.

When to Hospitalize the Suicide Ideator

We have discussed the importance of being alert to any disruptions in the therapy relationship with the suicide ideator. Research has shown that one of the issues that may create hopelessness in the ideator and, therefore, move them to completion would be some type of detrimental event in the therapy alliance. Certainly premature and unwarranted hospitalization could be considered disruptive of the therapy alliance. There are certainly times when the suicidal client creates in the therapist uncomfortable levels of anxiety. Unfortunately there are times where the therapist manages his or her own anxiety via interventions that are therapeutically inappropriate. One would be inappropriate hospitalization. Nevertheless, we do need to respect the fact that there are times when a suicide ideator could benefit from inpatient services. I would like to offer a very brief protocol that can be used by clinicians to determine if the individual in their setting, who is currently talking about suicide and is meeting the criteria for suicidal ideation could benefit from inpatient services. We need to recall, again, the exact criterion for suicidal ideation. These are men and women, young or old, who have recently experienced a tragic event or who have been dealing with a chronic painful condition. This event or condition is causing them unbearable levels of psychological/psychiatric pain. This pain currently defies their capacity to cope and because of their inability to manage this pain they begin to contemplate death as a solution. To determine when this population would benefit from inpatient safety, the following questions should be asked:

1. *What makes suicide an attractive alternative at this time?*

Probe for the perspective that recognizes suicide as a problem-solving strategy. I often frame the suicide wish in my clients as their desire to solve a problem. What you hope to hear in this pursuit is the client talking to you about their pain. You want to encourage them to be as clear and comprehensive as possible in this area. Remember Edwin Shneidman's admonition: "The first task of therapy is to identify the locus of the client's pain" (1985, p.40). This form of questioning allows you to identify not only where your client hurts, but also gives you a key to where you are going to start your therapy. We are listening for metaphors of hopelessness (fatalistic despair) and helplessness (severe self-devaluation). Once again, we are reminded: Listen, listen, listen. If we hear a metaphor for these emotions, we may start to consider inpatient safety.

2. *What plans are in place?*

The next focus in this evaluation is to discuss with the client any planning they have done and whether they have current access to lethal means. The rule here is quite simple: The more detailed the planning and accessible the means the more intense the intent to die. I will often ask my clients directly, "have you done any planning in response to your wish to die?" Remember, these are ideators and they are ambivalent about the wish to die. That ambivalence is in your favor as it motivates them to talk about their current issues.

3. *How does the thought of death make you feel?*

The third area of concern is a demonstrated or reported sense of calmness and peacefulness when thoughts of suicide or death are entertained. I will often ask my suicide ideators, "when you think about death, how does it make you feel?" I pay very close attention to feelings of peace and remember the quote from Nietzsche: "The thought of suicide is a powerful solace: by means of it one gets through many a bad night." In response to this question we hope to hear concern for loved ones, fear of death, anxiety, sadness. Be alert to expressed feelings of peace, calm, tranquility.

4. *What is keeping you alive?*

The final concern is to ask the client if they currently have anything in their lives keeping them from dying by suicide. We term this question: "looking for barriers." We make no judgments in this area. Anything the client subjectively defines as keeping them alive is to be respected. These barriers could be religious beliefs, fear of harming loved ones, fear of being seen as a coward, fear of a failed attempt. Remain alert to the client who clearly expresses language indicating no barriers. This language could be related to weakening ambivalence and inclination toward suicide. Also, remain alert to contingent barriers where the client indicates they will stay alive as long as a certain aspect in their lives does not change. Examples of these contingencies could be: "as long as my wife doesn't leave me" or "as long as I don't have to go to jail." These contingencies should be explored as they could be sources of pain or elements of manipulation.

Let me operationalize these questions by giving a few examples. I would like to talk about a young man whom I saw a number of years ago and his expression of suicidal ideation. He was in his late 20s, a referral from a drug court, and I had been seeing him for about two months on a weekly basis. Of concern during the time of one of our sessions was his current unemployment. He had just lost a well-paying job and with that he had also lost his health benefits. He was, therefore, unable to pay his court-mandated fee. We were involved, therefore, during this session in renegotiating his fee for the purpose of making him a *pro bono* client. In the middle of this conversation, this young man literally exploded. He proclaimed, in unmistakably clear language, that he was "tired of all this crap." He went on to tell me that he could no longer meet any of his financial obligations, he was at great risk of losing his house, and his girlfriend had just walked out on him. He explained that he had been sleeping very poorly, had no appetite, and his financial challenges occupied his mind throughout the day. He then looked at me and explained, "there are times I wish I was dead." I responded to this comment by asking him if he was thinking about suicide and he nodded in affirmation. I therefore proceeded to implement the protocol to determine if he was appropriate for inpatient services. The first question I asked him: "Why is suicide so attractive to you at this point in time in your life?" He responded by looking at me and proclaiming: "Everybody thinks about suicide at least once in their lives." He went on to say that it really didn't make any difference, because, "we are all going be dead anyway in five years from the avian flu." He then finished the comment by saying that nobody would miss him if he were dead anyway and, in fact, many people would be better off if he were dead. I then asked him if he had done any planning towards this goal of suicide and he responded by telling me that he had just purchased a gun. He added that he had chosen a location for his death, that he knew what he would wear, and that he had a CD that he was going to play at the time of his death. Ominously, he'd been writing notes to certain people. He told me that the reason he'd written notes was that he didn't want anybody to blame themselves for his decision. He then said to me that he hadn't sent a note out yet because, "something might change. I might get a job or I might win the lottery." This comment represents the shred of hope that makes him an ideator. The fact that he still had some hope things might change presents him with a brightened prognosis. It is this small flicker of hope that kept him from fatalistic despair and becoming a completer.

I then engaged with him on how he felt when he thought about his death. He responded to that by looking at me and saying that when he had picked up his gun from the gun store he brought the box into his car and unwrapped it. He said he took the gun in his hand, and then he said to me: "Holding a gun in my hand, knowing it was a way out of this pain, made me feel a peace I hadn't felt in weeks." I then asked him about barriers, anything that would keep him from dying from suicide, and he responded with, "no nothing at all." He continued, "I have no idea what happens when you die, heaven, hell, nothingness. All I do know is that whatever it is, it's got to be better than this."

I hospitalized that young man. The reason I did was that when I asked him about the goal of his suicide I heard metaphors for helplessness and hopelessness. The metaphor for hopelessness was when he told me that, "we're all going to be dead anyway in five years from the avian flu" and the metaphor for helplessness was when he began to talk about self-devaluation by stating that there would be some people who would be "better off" if he was dead. However, the basic reason I put him into the hospital was because of the specific planning. This young man had a gun, he had chosen a location, he knew what he was going to wear, he was writing suicide notes, and he was engaged in behaviors that one just cannot ignore. I also used, as a rationale for inpatient services, the fact that thoughts of suicide gave him a sense of peacefulness. And finally, he indicated that there were no barriers to his thinking about suicide. This young man was indeed an ideator; but, because of the criteria he met, I viewed him as very appropriate for inpatient services.

Another example is a 58-year-old woman that I met a number of years ago. She had just lost her husband of 34 years who had died of a heart attack on a Sunday morning leaving church. She was referred to me by her oldest daughter six weeks after her husband's funeral. Her daughter's concerns were that the client had not left her home in the six weeks since the funeral. The daughter also reported that the client had been drinking quite heavily since the funeral, and was talking about wanting to die. When she came into my office for her initial session she was very well dressed, very refined, alert and oriented but with a very subdued affect and mood. We talked for a few minutes and then I moved into the conversation to determine if she could benefit from inpatient services. I asked her why suicide and/or death was so attractive for her at this time in her life. She responded to me that since her husband's death she has been feeling a level of grief that she described as unbearable. She described this current unbearable level of grief as defying her capacity to cope and that her thoughts of death were basically designed to rid herself of the grief and to see her husband again. I asked her if she had given any thought to planning for her suicide. She told me that she did not have a gun and even if she did have a weapon she would not know how to use it. She then got me involved in a conversation around gun control policies on both the state and federal levels. I redirected her and asked her if she had given any thought or planning to any other method of taking her life and she then claimed that carbon monoxide poisoning was not an option because she could not tolerate the smell. She said to me that she cannot stand cigarette smoke much less carbon monoxide and then she began to engage with me in a conversation around the local non-smoking policies in force at the time. I asked her after this discussion if she had given any thought to how she would take her life and she responded with a clear "no." I then asked her that when she thought about her death how it made her feel. She told me it gave her a very powerful sense of peacefulness and tranquility, because the grief would be over with and she would see her husband again. But then she added that it also made her feel very sad, because she would miss her children, her grandchildren, and her friends. I then asked her if there were any barriers that were currently influencing her in her decision to die. She indicated that while she did think about death, she could never do it because she had seen what the loss of their father had done to her children and she could not do that to them. She also indicated that she belonged to a religious organization that teaches that if you die by suicide you spend eternity in hell. And then this very refined lady looked at me and said: "I do not want to spend eternity as a charcoal briquette."

I did not hospitalize this woman. She was very appropriate for outpatient treatment. The reason I did not hospitalize her was that I did not hear any messages of hopelessness or helplessness when discussing her goal of suicide. What I did hear was the exact nature of the suicidal ideation. She told me about the crisis. She told me about her unbearable pain, her inability to cope, and the option of death as a problem-solving strategy. Another reason I did not feel that she was appropriate for inpatient services was because she had given very little thought to planning the suicide. I also took into consideration the fact that when she thought about her death although it gave her a sense of peacefulness, it also made her feel very sad. We need to be alert to the fact that when thoughts of suicide are entertained they often do give a sense of peace, but we also hope to hear that it creates some type of aversive emotional reaction. Finally, I refrained from utilizing inpatient services because this woman had very powerful barriers. The barrier of what his or her death would do to the children is perhaps the most powerful barrier protecting an ideator from completed suicide. The religious and/or spiritual barrier is also a very important barrier for clinicians to pay attention to. I, therefore, continued to see her in therapy all the while monitoring the level of her ideation and being alert to any issues of hopelessness and helplessness, planning for suicide, overwhelming sense of peace when thoughts of death are entertained, and the loss of those powerful barriers.

Assessment to be Used at Intake to Elicit a History of Suicide Attempts

For years research has urged us to develop a format to assess whether a client that we are seeing has a history of suicide attempts. This format is ideally used during intake when we are seeing our client for the very first time. The purpose of this format and the reason for its importance is that a positive history for suicide attempts is a very powerful indicator of eventual death by suicide. The reader is reminded, however, to remember the exact nature of what goes in to a suicide attempt. Therefore, I would like to offer a format that can be utilized in a very simple fashion during intake for the purposes of determining if this person that you're seeing for the very first time has a history of suicide attempts.

1. *Can you give me a history of any suicide attempts?*

It is very important to begin the conversation with open-ended questioning. Avoid close-ended, "data retrieval" questioning. Close-ended, data retrieval questioning has been found to be extremely vulnerable to false positive responses. You are much more likely to receive a valid response if open-ended questioning is utilized. Therefore, avoid questions such as: "Have you ever made a suicide attempt?" What makes this a close-ended, data retrieval question is that it can be answered with one or two words. The goal is to encourage the client to talk with us. Close-ended, data retrieval questioning is not conducive to conversation. So we suggest beginning our conversation with the open-ended question of: "Can you give me a history of any suicide activity in your life?" That is an open-ended question which encourages conversation and communication from a client. You will find the client engaging with you in a comfortable, valid fashion.

If the client responds affirmatively to this first question, then the format is continued. The next question is to ask the client: "What did you do?" It is important to discover the lethality of the means and the reversible or irreversible nature of the activity. Using a firearm, for instance, will be of greater concern than an individual who reports to randomly swallowing an undetermined amount of pills.

2. *Why are you still alive?*

After the client reveals the method chosen to end his or her life, the next question to explore is the circumstances of the rescue. I encourage asking the client: "Can you help me understand why you are still alive?" The client's answer to this question will give you the information you need to determine if the act fits into one of the three categories defining the suicide attempt: 1) accidentally rescued against their wishes; 2) self-interrupted during a panic; or 3) miscalculated the lethality of the means. This is the vital question in this interview and will give you the information needed to determine if the client has a history of suicide attempts. If the client has attempted suicide in the past, the clinician will then ask a fourth question.

3. *What was going on in your life at that time?*

This question will focus on the condition(s) present when the attempt was made. When the client reveals to you what was happening to them at that time, be alert to the locus of pain. Once that locus of pain is discovered, it will be essential to discover if the situation has been resolved or if it remains a concern. If the client reveals that the condition that created the wish to die is still a major concern, then that issue becomes the focus of therapy.

Let me give you an example of how this format is implemented. I had an opportunity a number of years ago to meet a young woman in her early 20s who self-referred to my practice because of depression. During our intake process, I asked her if there was any history of suicidal activity in her life, and she responded that a number of years ago she made a suicide attempt. Because of that response I then continued the protocol by asking her what she did in the attempt to end her life. She responded very briefly with: "I tried to bleed to death by slashing my wrists." I then asked her the key question as we explore the circumstances of rescue: "Can you help me understand why you are still alive?" She indicated to me that the night of her attempt she was in college at a very small liberal arts school. The night of her attempt the entire student body was down in the school's auditorium for an event. Therefore, she said, "I felt safe in my attempt to bleed to death." Then she added that her roommate, who was in the auditorium, had forgotten her camera. When she returned to the dormitory to retrieve her camera she found my client lying on the floor bleeding profusely. The roommate called 911 and saved her life. With that response I was immediately able to classify this client as a person who is positive for a history of suicide attempts. If the roommate had not forgotten her camera there, would have been a high probability that this young lady would have died. I, therefore, have to be quite cautious and alert to this client since a history of suicide attempts is a very powerful correlate to eventual death by suicide. Furthermore, because she did have a history of suicide attempt activity, I asked about what was going on in her life at that time. She went on to tell me that she was an above-average student. She told me that in her entire academic career from elementary through high school she had received nothing but straight A's. The afternoon of the suicide attempt she received notice that she had received a B in one of her courses. This grade, at that moment in time, was psychologically intolerable for this young woman and, perhaps impulsively, she decided that the only way to end her pain was to take her life. I asked her if this anxiety over her academic performance was still an issue in her life and she indicated that it was. Through this very brief questioning I was able to identify the locus of her pain and also a focus for our work together.

This format, therefore, can be of extreme value in learning about our client. But, most importantly, when we do have a client with a history of suicide attempts, and we explore that history, we can discover quite a bit about their pain and often may discern a sense of direction in our therapy.

Assessment of the Intent and Lethality of the Suicide Completer

We talked earlier about the complicated and dangerous profile of the suicide completer—men and women who die by suicide. They are defined in various ways. There are, however, commonalities among them. They have a cognitive awareness that the activity they are ready to engage presents a significant risk of ending in their death. Indeed, their goal is death. This is the essential component of the definition of suicide. An act cannot be termed a suicide unless there was, on the part of the deceased, a clearly established *intent* to die. And, finally, suicide completers will, more often than not, engage in highly lethal means to assure that outcome. From data gathered by psychological autopsies and death certificates it is known that the profile of the suicide completer is usually as follows:

- Male
- Caucasian
- Living alone
- Unemployed
- Experiencing a mood, anxiety, or psychotic disorder
- Self-medicating with drugs
- Not in therapy at the time of their death
- Did not talk about suicide directly (may, however, speak about death through metaphors)
- Visited their primary care physician within six months of their suicide

In 2007 (Alexopoulos), there was an article in the *Journal of Advancing Suicide Prevention* on the tragic suicide of Bob Stern. The story of his death captures many of the elements contained in this lethality profile. It led the author of this article to address primary care physicians and their important role in identifying suicide completers. The author commented: "Routine assessment of suicidal ideation and/or intent in patients is necessary as these patients will rarely explicitly inform their physicians about suicidal thoughts or plans." The article goes on to state that potentially suicidal patients are passing through the offices of internists, family practitioners, and other primary care providers in droves, often unbeknownst to physicians and their staff. In fact, as many as 70 percent of patients who die by suicide have seen their primary care physician within a month of their death and 20 percent of them within a week of when they died. Robert Stern was one of these. This successful 77-year-old businessman had seen his doctor three days before he killed himself. The physician had even telephoned Bob within hours of the suicide to reassure him about an operation that he was scheduled to undergo the following day. What the doctor didn't know was that his phone call to Mr. Stern came at a very inopportune time. Bob was in the midst of videotaping a goodbye message to his family. Rather than be candid with his physician about his suicidal thoughts and plans, Bob reassured the doctor that all was well. He took his life no more than an hour after this phone call was concluded.

In my own practice I have had many experiences with the dynamics of this profile, especially the dynamic of "no intent communication." Many years ago my practice conducted a Survivors of Suicide support group. This was a group, which met every other week, for men, women and children who had lost a loved one to suicide. One evening a grieving pair of parents, who had lost their 28-year-old son to suicide, brought in a tape which had been made by their son right before his suicide. They wanted me to review the tape to determine if it would be appropriate to play for the group members at our next meeting. I did review the tape and felt it would be very appropriate for the group to hear their son's last comments before his death. The tape started with their son saying goodbye to the family. His voice was subdued, quiet and he sounded very sad and depressed, but his words were soothing, loving and calm—designed to alleviate any sense of guilt or responsibility that the family might have had as a result of his choice. In the middle of the tape, the phone rang. He left his taping for a few minutes to answer the phone, but he left the recorder on and it captured his phone conversation. It was his grandmother who was calling. In his conversation with his grandmother he appeared to be quite enthusiastic, happy, verbal and engaging. He talked to his grandmother about his wish to buy a new car, looking for a new job, and many other issues that were going on in his life. Finally, he mentioned to his grandmother that he had to be going and said to her as he concluded the conversation, "Remember Grandma, I love you and I will see you on Sunday for dinner." After the phone call was concluded he went back to the tape and, for one final moment, said a tearful goodbye to his family and then you heard the gunshot. No more than 30 seconds before this young man terminated his existence he said to his grandmother: I love you Grandma and I will see you on Sunday for dinner.

It may appear, from this information, that identifying the suicide completer in advance is a difficult, if not almost impossible, task. It is a challenge. There are a number of behaviors that we need to be aware of in our efforts to recognize and capture the suicide completer population. First of all, usually within six weeks of the suicide act, they experience significant psychological and/or psychiatric turmoil. Eating habits will change, sleeping habits will change. They will be more irritable than usual. They may have a significant difficulty in concentration, and their symptoms of depression, anxiety, and/or psychosis will become greatly enhanced. They will often verbalize hopelessness and helplessness. The reader is encouraged to remain alert to metaphors of fatalistic despair and significant self-devaluation which are the two primary ingredients to the emotions of hopelessness and helplessness. It is also known that prior to the suicide act that completers present with anhedonia and dysphoria. Anhedonia is a demonstrated inability to gain pleasure from behaviors that, at one time, had given the person pleasure. Adolescent males, for instance, demonstrate this when they give away prized possessions prior to their deaths. Often the adolescent male, as he is giving his best buddy his baseball card collection, will say: "I wanted you to have my baseball cards, I don't care about them anymore." Dysphoria is literally an emotional shutdown. Edwin Shneidman (1985, p.101), told us many years ago that men and women who die by suicide "die emotionally before they die physically." Suicide completers also will demonstrate a morbid preoccupation with the past. This will oftentimes be the person's recounting of a life full of regrets. It is quite often the only thing that they can talk about. They will discuss regrets over choosing the wrong profession, not saving enough money, not being a good parent, not being a good enough spouse or partner. They also, on occasion, will provide us with "remote suicide communication." This remote suicide communication will often be metaphoric. It will be phrased as a current apathy towards life and anticipation of death. For instance, they will often claim: "Life sucks and it wouldn't bother me at all if I got hit by a beer truck tomorrow." And, finally, they often will demonstrate a refusal to seek help when encouraged by friends or family members. Indeed, in over 40 years as a practitioner I have lost four clients to suicide. Two of those clients took their lives well after I had concluded therapy with them. One young man took his life about eight years after we concluded therapy and another young man took his life about 10 years after we concluded therapy. On both occasions their families urged them to come back and see me, and they both refused. When these behaviors are observed, it is essential that a safety setting be pursued. More often than not this safety setting should be a psychiatric inpatient facility. What is most important is that we avoid a practice that used to be called "the circle of surveillance." This was a practice, encouraged many years ago, where the at-risk person was watched by friends and family members on a 24-7 basis. It didn't work. The result was too often a guilt-ridden survivor who was "on duty" when the person died. We never put onto family or friends a job that is better done by a crisis center or an inpatient facility.

However, the most significant and lethal of all of these markers is the rapid change from turmoil to peacefulness and tranquility. It has been referred to, in various circles, as the "amazing reversal." It is a very rapid change from the turmoil spoken of above to a state of tranquility, calmness, and peacefulness. It will be during this time that the client will deny any suicidal intent and will not display any of the behaviors of concern. For the therapist, this dynamic could become your worst nightmare. Let me give you an example.

Many years ago I received a phone call from the mother of a young man in his late 20s. She was calling me out of concern for her son who she said had just been released from a psychiatric inpatient hospital. Apparently, he was released only because his insurance benefits had run out. She was concerned that his discharge was premature, and she was very concerned that he was still at risk. According to this mother, the family had hospitalized her son about a week before, because he was severely depressed over the breakup of a long-term relationship. The reason for her phone call was to find out if he still needed hospitalization and whether there was any way to hospitalize him regardless of his insurance problems. I spoke to her for a while about a number of different options and then she asked me if I would be willing to see her son to determine if he still needed hospitalization. I told her to have him give me a call. About one hour later this young man called me and we arranged for an appointment later on that afternoon. The young man showed up for his appointment in a timely fashion, dressed appropriately for the weather. His mental status exam was uncomplicated: He was oriented to time, place, person, and reason for interview. His thoughts were logically and coherently presented and eye contact was excellent. His affect and mood were congruent with circumstances. He had excellent futuristic thinking and, overall, the one hour and 45-minute interview appeared, on the surface, to be non-problematic. Throughout the entire interview he denied any current suicide ideation or intent and proclaimed significant optimism about his relationship with his girlfriend. As I have gone over this case many times in my mind over the years the one issue that for me significantly stands out was the fact that he presented as being "almost too good." I did have a sense of unease over his presentation and I commented in the mental status exam about my concern around the validity of his presentation.

During our conversation I asked the young man for permission to talk with his mother. He refused this request and indicated that later on he was going to have dinner with his family and he would tell his mother about our conversation. He added that if she had any further concerns she and I could talk at a later time. I also asked him for permission to talk to the hospital for information about his week-long stay at that facility. He refused this request also. He told me that since the hospitalization, he had been feeling much better, had no suicide intent, and was quite optimistic about the future. He also commented on the positive effects of his current medication. He was especially enthusiastic and optimistic about a fresh start in his relationship with his girlfriend. Toward the end of our session, I confronted this young man. I told him it was my experience that right before men and women die by suicide they oftentimes appear very calm and peaceful. I told him that they present in a fashion that was similar to the way he was presenting to me that afternoon. I then told him if that was the situation I hoped he would give therapy a chance. I encouraged him to see me on a regular basis and promised him that we would do our best to find a resolution to whatever was going on in his life that was problematic. This young man responded to this not so subtle confrontation by thanking me for my concern. He said, however, that he was feeling much better and he emphasized to me again that he had no suicidal intent and, finally, that he did not need therapy at this time in his life. At that point our session ended, I gave him my card and encouraged him to call. Approximately four hours later, I received a phone call from the mother telling me that she had just been notified that her son had died in his garage from a self-inflicted gunshot to the head.

This young man represents a classic example of the amazing reversal. As I mentioned, it could present the clinician with a significant challenge. In most states in order to place an individual citizen in a psychiatric facility against their will, a very specific process must be pursued. That process includes a recognition that the individual person is demonstrating behaviors associated with a mental disorder. Further, because of those mental disorders the person must be seen as dangerous to self, dangerous to others, or unable to care for personal needs. If we observe such behaviors, we are mandated to begin the process of involuntary hospitalization. During this one hour and 45 minute interview, this young man, unfortunately, gave me no information that could fit that criterion. The message here is quite clear: The earlier we capture the suicide completer, the more enhanced our outcome may be. If we delay our interventions to a point where the amazing reversal becomes a reality, the outcome may be tragic.

As we conclude this chapter, I would like to summarize some of the more important features we have discussed. In all assessments, whether it be for the ideator, the attempter, or the completer, it is essential to remember we assess people and not behaviors. It is encouraged, therefore, that when standardized tests and measurements are used for assessment purposes, they only be used to validate or invalidate our clinical judgment. We should never rely on a standardized test or measurement as a stand alone assessment. Our interview style should rely primarily on an open-ended question format. We should avoid using close-ended, data retrieval formats. The style of open-ended questioning is conducive to engaging the client in conversation.

As we assess people, it is our goal to get that person to talk to us. If all we ask is closed-ended, data retrieval questions, we limit the conversation the client can give to us.

I am often asked, "what should be done if a client lies to you?" That is a fascinating question. Another purpose, goal, and benefit of open-ended questioning is that it enhances the validity of our clients' responses. In an opposite fashion, close-ended, data retrieval questioning is very vulnerable to fabricated or false responses. The young man that I just spoke of literally lied to me for one hour and 45 minutes. I had no control over that, but I did my very best to engage him in a more revealing conversation. However, due to the dynamics of the amazing reversal, he was not about to divulge his plan for suicide at that time. His mind was made up, his plan was settled, and he was not going to allow anybody to interfere with his goal. His fabrications during our conversation were goal-oriented. The goal was to keep me from interfering with this plan.

Assessments are not designed to predict suicide. Assessments are designed, primarily, to gain insight into risk factors that a client may present. It is extremely important for clinicians to remember that society does not expect us to predict the future. What society does expect of us is to assess risk factors for specific behaviors. After the tragic death of that young man, I was brought in to litigation by his family. During that time, I learned a lot about the litigation process. One of the more valuable lessons I learned was the basis of the litigation was not that the young man died from suicide, but instead, it was based upon my competence. The question was presented in court: "Did I competently exercise my professional responsibilities?" The answer to that question was: "Yes, I did competently exercise my professional responsibilities. I had no control over that client's behavior. What I did have control over was the exercise of my job responsibilities." It was shown to the court that I had done my job. The mother asked me for an assessment and that's exactly what I did. The court found me not liable during this litigation process because I did the job society expects me to do. That is not only what society expects of us, but also what we should expect of ourselves. We, as professionals, need to be cautious about the expectations and burdens we, sometimes unfairly, place upon ourselves. We also need to be alert to, what has oftentimes been called, "fear-of-litigation-therapy." That is a process where the clinician acts towards a client in ways that are designed to protect themselves from potential litigation. It may, or may not, be what is good for the client and, unfortunately, is designed to take care of the therapist. In some instances, it could be conceived as a direct violation of our Hippocratic Oath.

And finally, of course, hindsight into suicide is always 20/20. But, before the act of suicide, life for our client and certain behaviors they perform are unique to them. Indeed, many situations in which individuals may appear suicidal do not necessarily result in completed suicides. Ronald Maris (1966, p.73) commented: "One might cynically conclude that the only suicide predictor is suicide itself." But we do the best we can. It is what society expects of us and what we should expect of ourselves.

CHAPTER FOUR

Guidelines For Treatment

A t one time or another most clinicians and therapists are faced with the prospect of engaging with a suicidal patient. Studies of stress among therapists indicate that the two most extreme stresses are a patient's suicide attempts and/or threats of suicide activity (Hellman, Morrison, and Abramowitz, 1986; Roswell, 1988). Our final chapter is devoted, therefore, to this most important issue – treating the suicidal and self-mutilating patient. I would like to offer a theoretical perspective. There are a number of guidelines that act as commonalities to all therapeutic approaches for this population. Some readers may be behaviorists; while others may be more psycho-dynamically oriented. Whatever the inclination, it is important to address the essential concepts of treatment.

Discover the Pain. Edwin Shneidman (1985, p. 40) tells us: "The first task of therapy is to discover the locus of the client's unbearable pain and to decrease the perturbation associated with that condition." We go to the client's pain. That pain is idiosyncratically defined by the client. The level of pain may be so severe that it defies the person's capacity to cope. Suicide, therefore, becomes a coping strategy for unbearable pain. It can be argued that men and women vulnerable to suicide are those who have weakened coping abilities. Studies reveal that suicidal individuals are unlikely to have the ability to tolerate the emotional, interpersonal, and behavioral stresses in their lives. They appear to have significant difficulties consisting of cognitive rigidity, lacking in ability to

95

deal with abstracts, dichotomous thinking, gaining insight from previous life experiences, dependent personalities, significant indecisiveness, and a vulnerability to surrender into hopelessness (Linehan, 1987; Fawcett, 1988). Suicidal behaviors are viewed as problem-solving behaviors and are, of course, the ultimate escape from the problems of this life.

The therapist, therefore, has the task and responsibility to enhance the client's coping; or, to make the unbearable pain, a bearable pain. Essentially, we are encouraged to pay minimal attention to suicide as a behavior and to focus our efforts on strengthening our patient's ability to manage life's problems. I will often reframe a client's suicidal ideation as "their wish to solve a problem." We dedicate our efforts in therapy to enhance our client's struggle to remain alive. Our goal is to move our client to experience life as something they can control and manage in a way that is productive.

All Behaviors are Purposeful. Linehan (1993) urges us:

> It is of critical importance to determine whether suicidal behavior is primarily respondent behavior, operant behavior, or both. Behavior is respondent when it is automatically elicited by a situation or specific stimulus event. The behavior is under the control of the preceding events and often it is impulsive. With respect to suicidal behavior, the behavioral paradigm here is that of "escape learning." (p.163)

That is, suicidal responses are viewed as escape behaviors elicited by aversive conditions, such as traumatic events or physical or emotional pain. When Shneidman proposes that the universal precipitant of suicidal behavior is unbearable pain, he is proposing that suicidal behavior should be conceived as respondent. Suicidal ideation and urges elicited by extreme panic or by explosive anger are examples.

Operant behaviors function to affect the environment. When suicide, suicide attempts, and suicidal ideation and threats function to reunite a person with dead loved ones or to elicit care or guilt, or to get into a hospital, and so on the behavior is functionally operant. The notion of suicidal behavior as a "cry for help," popularized by Shneidman and Farberow (1986), is an example of suicidal behaviors as operant (Linehan, 1993).

It is extremely important that the therapist not assume that suicidal behavior is operant or respondent. Assessment is crucial. Neither theory nor the patient's diagnosis can answer this question, only careful observation can. Much of the time, suicidal behaviors, especially chronic suicide attempts and suicide threats, are simultaneously respondent and operant. Hopelessness, despair, and the unbearable pain of life elicit these behaviors. The community response, for example, getting help, taking the person seriously, taking the person out of a difficult situation, taking responsibility for the person, and/or providing care for the person, reinforces this behavior. An essential part of therapy is to assist clients in recognizing the respondent and/or operant goals of their behaviors. This focus will assist the therapist in the client's recognition of their goals and a direction for therapy. Once these patterns become clear to the client the therapist can focus attention on helping the client learn how to handle problematic situations in a more effective fashion and how to generate desired outcomes in non-suicidal ways. Suicidal individuals often see no way out of their problems except suicide. Our function, therefore, is to expand the client's options, or as Shneidman tells us, "remove their blinders" and provide them with other ways to solve problematic situations, even those situations that are accompanied by seemingly unbearable pain.

We Treat People Not Behaviors. I mentioned earlier in this book that I learned a very valuable lesson early in my career that has been a guidepost for my actions with clients. That lesson was given to me by a very wise gentleman who told me, in reference to a client that I was working with who had significant substance dependency, that we don't treat addiction disorders we treat people with addiction disorders. While that may seem to be a very simplistic statement it is, in reality, very profound. At times we find ourselves engaged in a pattern of therapy designed only to change our client behaviors. In that devotion, we may miss some significant and critical information about who that client is and how he or she comes to be in our presence. On this subject I would urge all readers to devote themselves to the term "case conceptualization." Donald Meichenbaum (2009, p.3) has told us that "therapy without an appropriate case conceptualization is like a ship without a rudder. It wanders aimlessly with no sense of direction." Case conceptualization is the absolute essential element in treatment planning. Case conceptualization is, basically, getting to know the client. What are the essentials in developing an appropriate case conceptualization?

The first feature is an in-depth examination of the client's strengths and weaknesses. Questions related to social support, problem solving, coping strategies, and motivation for treatment are of vital importance. The therapist is urged to look at issues of resiliency, hope, self-regard and basic issues such as housing, education, employment, legal history, relationship history. The next key feature of case conceptualization is a thorough exploration of long-term and short-term goals. What does the client need at this time in his or her life? An example of a short-term goal would be the cessation of behaviors of self-harm or suicide intent. Long-term goals are aligned with the client's hope for a "life worth living" (Linehan, 1993). Short-term goals are, ideally, brief, specific and measurable. The long-term goals, on the other hand, will be ambitious, hopeful and comprehensive. In the theory of case conceptualization, the therapist addresses the client's strengths and weaknesses in the attainment of these goals. These goals are defined by the client and respond to their current life situation. The therapist acts as a "stimulator" in providing thoughts that the client may use to determine the goals. The benefit of this process is that these goal-oriented activities allow the client to acquire a sense of "ownership" of the therapy and promotes the therapy as a "hope-providing" relationship. Every long-term goal should have a series of shorter term goals that will be used to move the client towards accomplishment of it. The more ambitious the long-term goal, the more short-term goals may need to be developed.

The concept of case conceptualization incorporates the therapist's encouraging the client to "tell their story." Everybody has a story. The therapy relationship often begins with the simple question of "tell me about yourself." Clients may react to that query with a need for clarification. They may often ask for a sense of direction. The therapist would want information on the client's social context, environmental needs, occupational/vocational definition, psychological/psychiatric issues, developmental history, medical concerns, legal involvement, and other issues that the therapist feels would give a comprehensive picture of this unique person currently seeking assistance.

Always Be Where The Client Is. This essential is often referred to as "stage of change-specific interventions." It is based on the theories of Prochaska, Norcross and DiClementi, (1994). Their concept of the stages an individual experiences as he or she embarks upon behavioral change is not only valuable for marking client progress, but it also provides significant guidelines for where to start therapy and on what issues we should tread with caution. The assessment of the client's readiness to change is of vital importance. We never want to get "trapped" going to an issue where the client is in significant resistance. This resistance may be manifested by the client in a variety of ways. Prochaska et al, tell us that resistance is the *Pre-Contemplation Stage of Change*. This stage is the first stage of change, and the therapist needs to be aware of, and respectful of, this manifestation. In the pre-contemplation stage of change clients may present in a variety of ways. They may, for instance, present as rationalizing their behaviors. They are vulnerable to projecting blame onto other people, denying responsibility for their actions, or finding significant benefits to their current behaviors. They are inclined to engage the therapist in a format of debate. If we are not cautious, we can easily be trapped in this format. The client may also present, in the pre-contemplation stage of change, as fearful or reluctant to change. These are clients who, for better or worse, feel a certain comfort level in coping with extremely dysfunctional or maladaptive conditions. The safety they feel in their current coping may present the therapist with significant challenges in motivating them to change behaviors. We are also confronted on certain occasions with the rebellious client. These are men and women who are very familiar with controlling relationships through hostility. They are recognized by consistently confronting us by questioning our expertise and doubting the validity of our suggestions. A final form of resistance is the resigned client. These are men and women who, quite often, have a history of multiple exposures to treatment. Sadly, throughout these exposures nothing has changed for them, and they become quite hopeless about ever being able to change. These are the most notable expressions of resistance we find in our clients. When we discover that our client is in the pre-contemplation stage of change we have one task: Establish the therapeutic relationship. This is accomplished by effective listening, reflecting empathy, getting to know the client, encouraging them to talk about themselves, and identifying the locus of their pain. This is

essential for clients in the pre-contemplation stage of change –
listen and identify the locus of pain.

Once the locus of pain has been identified we now move the
client to the *Contemplation Stage of Change*. This is the stage where,
with our assistance, the client begins to explore the identified
locus of pain. We need as much information as possible. We
need to explore with the client its origins, its symptoms, and its
social, vocational, occupational, and relational consequences. In
other words, we need as much information about this identified
locus of pain as the client is capable of giving us. It is, however,
vitally important that we do not allow the client to remain in this
stage of change for a prolonged period. It is often claimed that
the contemplation stage of change is a vitally important place
to visit but you do not want the client to live there. Once the
clinician has enough information about the locus of the client's
pain it is strongly encouraged that we move on to the next stage
of change, the preparation stage of change.

The Preparation Stage of Change is often called the fundamental
aspect to treatment. The preparation stage of change is the
period of time in the therapy relationship that is devoted to
discussions on strategies that the client may consider. We will
engage with the client in a discussion around multiple strategies.
As we examine this menu of enhanced coping we will explore
the benefits and drawbacks of each strategy. We will devote more
time to this stage of change later in this chapter when we talk
about the structure of a treatment plan. Once the therapist feels
that an appropriate number of strategies have been explored and
examined, one strategy will be chosen for the client to take into
their real-world and experiment as to its efficacy for them. We
will then be moving the client into the next stage of change, the
Action Stage of Change.

The Action Stage of Change is the stage of experimentation. This is a critical stage of change because it is here that we provide the client with the continuous, hope-providing relationship and we also develop resiliency. The client is now encouraged to go back into their environment, away from the safety of the therapy relationship, and implement the skills learned during the preparation stage of change. There is no failure in this stage of change. If a strategy that we implement does not work then we will try another. This is why it is so all-important during the preparation stage of change to discuss a menu of enhanced coping strategies. It is in the action stage of change where resiliency is developed.

Resiliency has been defined in a variety of ways but it is, essentially, the ability to bounce back from adversity. Therefore, during the action stage of change if one of our enhanced coping strategies does not appear to be successful we will either scrap the strategy entirely or we will redefine and retool it based upon the lessons we learned. This strategy also helps to develop the continuous, hope-providing relationship. The spirit of the therapy relationship is focused on never giving up. We will always be capable of examining and exploring further enhanced coping strategies.

The Role of Motivation. Nobody changes behaviors without motivation. This is the key element in successful therapy. We have talked at length about the vital importance of identifying the locus of the client's pain. It will oftentimes be that pain will act as the motivation for the client to engage in behavioral change. In their wonderful publication, Miller and Rollnick (2002), speak at length about the strategies utilized to move the client to motivation. They tell us "intrinsic motivation for change arises in an accepting, empowering atmosphere that makes it safe for the person to explore the possibly painful present in relation to what is wanted and valued." (Miller & Rollnick, 2002, p.14) They tell us that motivation for change is the result of an interaction between people. Stressing that it is the result of an interpersonal process and therefore they emphasize the importance of the relationship in therapy. They also stress that in this relationship authoritarian coercion, however subtle, is never used. Most importantly is that motivation for change must come from the client and not be imposed by the therapist. We need to be extremely alert and cautious about this as there are times where we may use "emotional blackmail" under the guise of motivating our clients. Arguments for change in behavior should come from the client. This motivation for change, therefore, also comes from within the client. They also state that the client must remain autonomous throughout the entire therapy relationship. I am oftentimes asked, for instance, "what do you do when a client lies to you?" In response to that question I stress the importance of respecting the client's autonomy. If, at this time in therapy, the client decides to lie to me, that is his or her decision. This frame is also important in that it allows us to approach the therapy relationship as one of mutuality. Often therapists find themselves doing all the work, but it is essential that both the therapist and the client share the responsibility of the therapy's outcome. We respect that motivation for change is the responsibility of the client and not the therapist's responsibility.

There are a number of guiding principles for the establishment of this relationship. The first is to respect the fact that when we are working with a resistant client the resistance is never opposed. We are encouraged to roll with this resistance. We do not want to be trapped by resistance. You do not want to get stuck in the client's pre-contemplation stage. While we are not agreeing with the client's resistant behavior, we are accepting of it. We accept the behavior and we move on. The next guiding principle is to ensure that the relationship is based upon respectful listening. In order to establish a relationship where it is safe for the client to explore their possibly painful present, it is of fundamental importance to be a good listener. During this period of time we express empathy and acceptance of our client's perspective of their life. What we are listening for is the client to touch on their pain. This pain is defined as some type of psychiatric, psychological, or social turmoil that is perceived by the client as a discrepancy between current behaviors and personally-valued goals and wishes. The authors stress that without this discrepancy there is no pain and without pain there is no motivation to change. We mentioned above that without this pain there is no movement from the pre-contemplation stage of change to the contemplation stage of change. This focus on the discrepancy is considered by the authors to be the most important aspect of the therapeutic relationship. We are also reminded, at this time, of Shneidman's quote that "the first task of therapy is to identify the locus of the clients' bearable pain and to decrease the perturbation associated with the condition" (1985). The final guiding principle for the establishment of this relationship is to be consistently alert for opportunities to enhance confidence in the patient's ability to change. We are consistently looking for chances to affirm our client. The belief is that if the client has an enhanced sense of responsibility for his or her own recovery and a sense of self-affirmation, their chances of recovery are greatly improved.

The Structure of the Treatment Plan

There are four major components to a treatment plan for the suicidal and self-harming client. This treatment plan will incorporate the basic guidelines listed above. We will then operationalize the plan by exploring a case study.

The Safety Plan. The first component of the treatment plan is to engage the client in a plan for safety. This is a verbal agreement between the client and the therapist. It is important to avoid written agreements that could take the form of a "contract." It is essential that we avoid any contractual language in the treatment plan, especially avoiding a dynamic that was called the "No Suicide Contract." This vehicle, which was developed in the 1970s, was a written agreement that the client was urged to sign—often with punitive consequences for non-compliance—which stated the client would not engage in any activity that would self-harm or be interpreted as a suicide activity. In 2007, Lewis, after extensive research on the matter, indicates:

> ...written contracts contain an initial statement in which the client agrees not to kill or harm themselves in any way...there is a signature line for both the client and the clinician. These contracts are often seen as standard procedures in mental health although there is no empirical evidence supporting their effectiveness and they do not protect clinicians from malpractice (as many believe). The regular use of these contracts should cease and clinicians should focus on safety plans that can guide clients when they are experiencing a crisis situation (216).

On the issue of malpractice and litigation—which often appears as the stimulus for these contracts—she states: "the issue here is the use of the word **contract**. Lawyers assume clinicians mean contract the same way they do, and clients are not competent to agree to a contract while suicidal. Therefore, a clinician could actually open oneself up to litigation, rather than avoiding a lawsuit" (Lewis, 2007, p.71).

Therefore, **the safety plan** is encouraged. This verbal agreement will include a client- and therapist-generated list of activities the client will engage in when there is an urge to self-mutilate and/or act on a suicide impulse. These activities may include an agreement to notify family members when there is a risk, to engage in an emotion-regulating activity, to avoid toxic situations, and to call the therapist and/or a crisis line when the client feels overwhelmed. The therapist will then document in the client's chart this verbal agreement. The client does NOT sign it. This verbal agreement should be visited and, if needed, revised during the relationship as circumstances dictate.

The Crisis Plan. This component is, basically, the Informed Consent. It is usually completed during the initial intake session and it will include informing the client of the circumstances during which confidentiality in the therapeutic relationship will be suspended. The therapist will explain these circumstances in very comprehensive and explicit terms. It will also be during this time that other "crisis-defined conditions" will be examined. For instance, under what circumstances would in-patient services be considered? What would lead the clinician to use legal resources to mandate hospitalization? Under what conditions would the clinician refuse to see the client (e.g., appearing for a session intoxicated). What are the clinician's personal boundaries (e.g., time frames for off-hours crisis contact and/or consequences of client's assaultive behaviors)? The important feature to this element of the treatment plan is that we never spring any surprises on our clients. They should be aware from the beginning of therapy of the clinician's obligations and boundaries (what we will and/or will not do and what we can and/or cannot do). This is a mutual function with the client's input and questions encouraged and respected. When completed, it is documented by the clinician and signed by the client to indicate they have been informed.

Problem Identification. The clinician gives a thorough description of the focus of treatment. Ideally, this will be the locus of client identified pain. It is important to recall that suicide is NOT a problem. Self-mutilation is NOT a problem. These behaviors are *problem management strategies*. The problems will be identified by the client as those issues causing unendurable pain and for which thoughts of suicide and/or self-mutilation provide temporary relief. It is essential that the clinician gain as much information about this identified problem as possible. It is also important that the client agree that this is the problem they wish to discuss. The clinician does not identify the problem. Often this identified problem may not be the reason the client was referred to the clinician. That is perfectly acceptable—the client knows where he or she hurts. Most often there will be a correlation between the locus of pain and the suicidal ideation and/or self-mutilation. The clinician's focus will be to assist the client in seeing this correlation (e.g., suicidal thoughts entertained for the purpose of eliminating an unbearable sense of loneliness). We assist the client in viewing suicide and self-mutilation as "ways of managing pain."

Problem Solving Strategies. Shneidman calls this "removing the client's blinders" (1985). The clinician wants to expand the client's problem-solving options. Suicide, suicidal thoughts, and self-mutilation often result from a significant lack of problem solving and coping strategies. It was mentioned earlier how important it is to identify and respect cognitive rigidity in our clients. This personal deficiency may lead to a vulnerability to suicide and self-mutilation as problem-solving strategies. It is the task of the therapy to offer the client a menu of alternative coping and problem-solving strategies that they may choose as alternatives to suicide and/or self- mutilation. Once we have identified the all-important locus of pain, we may want to engage with the client in a conversation on alternative coping. We will, as a matter of fact, often ask the client: "Would you like to spend some time with me looking at other ways you can manage your pain other than cutting or thinking about suicide?" We often reframe suicide and self-mutilation as: "your wish to solve a problem." Our hope is, that with appropriate motivation, the client will take us up on our offer. Our goal in therapy is to replace maladaptive coping with adaptive coping. Our goal is to assist the client in finding different ways of pain management. Our goal is not pain *elimination*. We cannot engage in a conversation with our client on this basis. We often find folks who want "the pain to go away." We can't do that. The client needs to know that we can't do that.

What do we teach? These skills may differ based on your professional inclination. That being said, it is advisable to begin with a behavioral approach. Our clients are in significant pain and are contemplating death. We may not have the luxury of time on our side that we would enjoy with the non-suicidal client. We need to teach, monitor, and encourage serious behavioral strategies that may result in a measurable reduction in life-threatening behaviors. There are some specific behaviors we would want to address immediately for the purpose of enhanced coping and a reduction in life-threatening behaviors.

First, is teaching our client how to pay attention to themselves (how to be mindful). Many clients are reactive. They act without contemplation of the events that lead to their situation. This feature of treatment is about going on a journey with the client. We want the client to pay attention to their lives and, most importantly, to their emotional reactions. The therapist will choose a recent critical event in the client's life and do an analysis of this event from a behavioral and emotional perspective. Linehan tells us that this analysis should be carried out in "excruciating, moment to moment detail" (Linehan et al., 1999). She further urges "the therapist should elicit enough detail to clarify the environmental events, emotional and cognitive responses, and overt actions that led to the suicidal response and/or episode" (Linehan et al., 1999).

The second treatment focus is to decide if the problem can be solved immediately. Not all problems can be solved in one or two sessions. There are times when the therapist may suggest to the client that one short-term solution to the current problem being discussed is to simply tolerate the painful consequences. The therapist must oftentimes teach the patient or the client to accept what cannot be immediately changed. This ability to tolerate stress is taught in the context of the therapeutic relationship. It is stressed to the client that this enhanced capacity to tolerate pain is a short-term solution. It is put into place when more viable problem-solving strategies have yet to be finalized.

The next treatment approach is to decide if the locus of the pain is primarily environmental, interpersonal, or emotional. The question that must be addressed is whether the client has the necessary skills to change their environment, improve interpersonal relationships, or learn emotional regulation skills. If the client does not have the skills to address these above-mentioned areas, then what does the individual need in this regard? Does the individual have the ability to change or improve his or her own emotional, environmental, or interpersonal functioning? The therapist will decide, based on the previously discussed case conceptualization, what the client's strengths and weaknesses are. Based upon that evaluation the therapist will decide, in as exact a fashion as possible, what skills the client would need to be taught.

Let's now operationalize these treatment principles by offering a case study. We would first give to you a brief case conceptualization of this client: A 43-year-old Caucasian male comes to the agency by order of the Drug Court in Kalamazoo, Michigan. He appears for the interview on time, dressed appropriately for the weather, and expresses an understanding of the purpose of the session. He presents as friendly, making good eye contact, displaying appropriate thought organization skills while not displaying any sign of bizarre or delusional thought content. His affect is flat, mood is dysphoric, and he uses an extreme economy of words when responding to the interviewer's comments. While significant agitation, restlessness, and irritability were not clinically observed during the interview; material presented later by the client's history validates the presence of those behaviors in current functioning. He displays an acceptable capacity for insight and empathy.

The client explains that he is here at the order of the drug court because of his second DUI in the last two years. He was placed on five-year probationary status, a restricted license for one year, charged over $2000.00 in fines, and ordered into treatment at an agency of his choice. His probation officer recommended this office for services. The client reveals that he is not happy with having to drive 60 miles one way to our office from his home. He relates that his probation officer is "out to get him" and "make my life miserable." But, he concludes, "at least I didn't get any time in prison."

The client reveals that he is married, has one child, a 14-year-old son, is currently unemployed and, due to that, is "close to filing for bankruptcy." When asked how this financial turmoil was affecting him and his family he stated, "I think we'll be fine if my wife would put some control on her spending habits" He went on to put the responsibility for the family's financial problems on his wife. When asked to provide further information on the unemployment issue he answered that he had worked for 20 years as a drug salesperson for a pharmaceutical company located in Kalamazoo, Michigan. He reports, in a rather matter-of-fact fashion, that his production numbers had "below expectations" for eight consecutive months, and he was fired. When asked to expand on the poor production numbers he replied, "I feel tired all the time, and I have no energy. I've gone to the doctor about this…they've done blood work…and can't find anything physically wrong with me." He reports that this lack of energy caused the poor production numbers which, in turn, led to his dismissal. He indicates little worry, however, over this issue and confidence that he will soon find other employment.

When asked to provide a history of his "tired feelings" he responds, "I think I have felt this way my whole life." When asked about previous services for mental health concerns, he glares at the interviewer and replies, "No! I'm not nuts." When asked if this chronic tired condition worries him, he responds with an affirming nod of the head. I ask the client about any history of suicide ideation, intent, or activity and he responds affirmatively. He claims to have "thought about it quite often in the last few weeks." He explains that "the situation at home" creates the wish to die. Then he added: "I would never do it, though. I couldn't do that to my son."

The client gives the following history of his alcohol use. He recalls first using alcohol at age 13 with friends. He becomes animated when recounting that the initial alcohol use made him feel "energized." He goes on to offer the insight that alcohol has had this energizing effect on him his entire life. He claims there have been significant benefits to alcohol use for him and, except for the current legal involvement, he does not see himself as an alcoholic nor does he view alcohol use a current problem. He also remarked on the "calming" effect that alcohol provides and that it actually provides "relief from stress" and "sometimes actually keeps me from killing myself." In response to an open query regarding family of origin, he responds with controlled anger regarding his father. "Now, there was an alcoholic," he stated strongly. He goes on to offer details regarding the physically and emotionally abusive nature of his childhood due, primarily, to his father's use of alcohol. He is the oldest in a sibship of three. Both biological parents are deceased. The father died early in life due to complications of excessive alcohol use.

He classifies his current marriage as "a disaster." He offers very few details other than to say that his wife and her family are at the root of many of the family's problematic issues. It does appear that his alcohol use is one of the issues that create periodic family turmoil. He adds to that revelation, however, that "just because they think I have a problem, doesn't make it a problem…maybe they should start looking at some of their problems and quit bothering me." When the conversation moves to discussing his relationship with his son his affect changes quickly to sadness. To an open offer to discuss this relationship, he states, "it's not good…but I love him so very much." He adds, "I wanted to be better…I just don't know what to do." He finishes his discussion of this issue with, "I always promised myself that I would raise my children better than I was raised…I feel I have failed."

This very brief case conceptualization provides significant information about the client which will be useful in the therapy endeavor. First of all, he makes it clear that he is self-medicating depression, anxiety, stress, and suicide ideation. He views alcohol as extremely important and beneficial, and he is not about to begin a conversation on abstinence. He has been self-medicating since early adolescence. We are accepting of that and move toward discovering his pain.

He has multiple stressors in his life. From the perspective of the multi-axial review of DSM-IV-TR, he has Axis I conditions of Alcohol Abuse, Depressive disorder NOS, Anxiety disorder NOS. From an Axis II view, he shows traits of Anti-Social Personality disorder. Axis III is his chronic fatigue and tiredness and, from Axis IV, he has financial, occupational, legal, primary support, access to health care, and parent/child conflict psycho-social stressors. He is highly defended on most every aspect of his situation. He views his alcohol use as very beneficial and he will not, at this time, look at his chronic depressive disorder (probably dysthymia) and anxiety disorder (possible GAD and/ or PTSD) as due to a psychological or psychiatric condition. Indeed, he looks at his chronic depression as a medical problem— which could be a contributing factor. He is also highly defended regarding his psychosocial stressors. He projects blame onto others, rationalizes his behaviors, denies responsibility, and sees benefits to his current maladaptive coping mechanisms. He is in the stage of pre-contemplation for virtually every issue in his life. In that stage of change, he would be seen as a *Rationalizing Client*.

In that first session, however, the client gives me "a gift." He talks to me about his locus of pain and an area where he is not defended and very raw. This lack of defense and rawness is contributing to his current suicide ideation. He tries to medicate this emotional issue but the "vicious cycle" takes hold. The more he drinks to defend himself the more damage is done to the father/son relationship. This, in turn, provokes more alcohol use. He does not see this right now, and it will be the therapist's challenge to arrange a treatment atmosphere that is nurturing of his discovery of this dynamic. He is capable of insight, and we have to trust his pain will provide the motivation toward this goal. In fact, with appropriate support, our hope is that this powerful discrepancy (the turmoil of the father/son relationship) will motivate him toward sobriety and reduce his suicide intent. Our initial goal here is to reduce the intensity of the suicide intent by allowing him some management over his relationship with his son. We are cautious on never demanding sobriety (we do not practice "abstinence-mandated therapy") prematurely. His alcohol use is medicating him and he is NOT motivated to abstinence. To demand immediate sobriety and abstinence would be to endanger the therapy alliance and to prematurely strip the client of a very important defense mechanism.

Let us now capture some brief conversations between this client and therapist from our first three sessions and examine how these goals are achieved.

The Precontemplation Stage Of Change

Interviewer: Good morning, glad you could make it in. This morning we are going to spend about an hour getting to know each other. Over time I'll be getting specific information, but for now you could start by telling me about yourself.

Client: Well, to tell the truth, I don't think there is anything to be concerned about. It is true that I now have two DUI's and am in some legal difficulty...but I don't see myself as an alcoholic. I was just too dumb to recognize that I shouldn't have been driving after drinking the way I did. Believe me...I am now a firm believer in taxi cabs. I'm just trying to say that just because I have two DUI's doesn't make me an alcoholic...I just used poor judgment.

Interviewer: You make a good point...your take on this is that a DUI doesn't mean you are addicted to alcohol. Can you give me an understanding of this legal difficulty you mentioned?

Client: Well, as I'm sure you know, I'm on probation for a few years...I had a $2000 fine...and I have driving restrictions...like driving to these appointments, driving to work, whenever I get another job, and driving to doctor's appointments...stuff like that. By the way, please don't take offense, but this probation officer sending me here to Grand Rapids when I live 60 miles away in Kalamazoo...that really busts my chops. You can't tell me they don't have any shrinks in Kalamazoo. That PO is out to get me.

Interviewer: I can understand the frustration with the travel. I will make every attempt to schedule your appointments at a convenient time for you. You are currently unemployed? Can you fill me in on that?

Client: I was working for Pharmacia's marketing division. I was a drug representative. My production numbers were below expectations for a couple of months and they let me go.

Interviewer: What's your take on the production numbers issue?

Client: Lack of interest…lack of drive…I get tired very easily. You know, that is a concern of mine…this tiredness I'm always feeling. I've been this way for as long as I can remember.

Interviewer: Have you discussed this with your doctor?

Client: Absolutely. They did all kinds of tests…blood work… everything.

Interviewer: Anything come up?

Client: No…I'm in perfect health. How about that…I've been drinking since I was 13 and I'm in perfect health. I think that's further proof that I'm not an alcoholic.

Interviewer: Well, I'm glad to hear you're in good health. Did the doctor talk about any possible emotional concerns regarding the tiredness?

Client: You mean like depression? No…I'm not nuts.

Interviewer: Yet, I can understand your concern.

Client: Yes…especially since I think it was the cause of my being fired.

Interviewer: Since the job loss, have there been any family concerns?

Client: Finances, of course. But we would still be in good shape if my wife would learn how to operate under a budget. I'm really not worried…I'm confident I'll find something soon.

Interviewer: Any other family concerns?

Client: You mean other than my wife and her family always on my back about my drinking?

Interviewer: I'm sure that can be stressful…they appear concerned about you.

Client: Listen…let me tell you something about my use of alcohol. I'm not a useless bum sleeping under a bridge because his brain is pickled. I have been a very successful professional for years, supported my family very well, and, until now, have been a model citizen. In fact, I think, to be quite honest, that alcohol helps me. It energizes me…makes me more social…I actually think clearer when I've had a few beers.

Interviewer: Right now you see more advantages to drinking than disadvantages.

Client: That's correct.

Interviewer: Can you help me understand the history of your alcohol use?

Client: What do you want to know?

Interviewer: Whatever you would like to share with me or anything you feel would help me understand better.

Client: Well, like I said, I started at 13…with my buddies. You know…stealing some of the old man's beer, sneaking into the garage…that kind of stuff.

Interviewer: How was that first experience?

Client: It was great. Really. I was always kind of a shy kid and I became the life of the party. But I was careful not to drink too much…I didn't want my mom to think I was drunk. She had enough to worry about with my dad. Now… he was an alcoholic.

Interviewer: Help me understand that.

Client: My father?

Interviewer: Yes…could you give me some information about him?

Client: Well, I'm not at all like him. He was a drunk and was brutal to my mom and his kids.

Interviewer: Brutal?

Client: When he was drunk he would use all of us as punching bags. I'm proud of the fact that I'm a different kind of father than he was.

Interviewer: You should be proud of that. In what way are you different from your father?

Client: I have a son…age 14. I love him beyond words. We were best buddies when he was little. I'd cut off my arms before I would lay a hand on him.

Interviewer: Your son is an important part of your life. Can we talk about your current relationship with your son?

Client: He's sullen and avoids me. We don't talk anymore. We don't do things together like we used to…because I'm so tired all the time. It has nothing to do with my drinking…I don't think. I don't know what's wrong or what to do.

Interviewer: This isn't the way you want it to be, is it?

Client: No…not at all. I can remember as a kid promising myself that if I ever became a dad….I would never be like my father… that my kids would love me…and I would love them.

Interviewer: This is very hard on you…your relationship with your son.

Client: Yes…I feel so guilty….

Interviewer: Can we talk more about that feeling?

Client: Guilt? I'm not the father I promised myself I would be…I feel I've failed.

Interviewer: You want to be a good father…would you like to talk some more about that?

Client: I thought I was here to talk about my DUI's.

Interviewer: This is your counseling session…we talk about what you want to talk about

Client: Well…I think it would help…I'd like to talk more about my son. These feelings of guilt are killing me. I just can't live like this.

Interviewer: Any thoughts on suicide?

Client: Yes…but I'd never do it…I couldn't do that to my son. The only time I don't think about it is when I've had a few beers.

Interviewer: Sounds like talking about you and your son would be important. Now, I'd like to summarize our session.

First, you have been very open with me and I appreciate that. You came here at the order of your PO and, in spite of the inconvenience and distance, you did appear. You're currently unemployed, have some financial challenges, you are dealing with legal issues, and appear to have some family turmoil. You are concerned about this chronic state of tiredness that may be the contributing factor to you losing your job. Alcohol use is currently not seen as a problem…in fact, you currently see some benefits to it. And, finally, I see you worried about your relationship with your son…and we can spend time talking about that. I'm also going to keep up to date on the suicide feelings.

I trust that you will tell me if they become overwhelming.

Commentary: This is a brief, albeit simple, dialogue sample of the Motivational Interviewing process of eliciting the discrepancy as a means for building motivation for change in a client in the pre-contemplation stage of change. Most of the interviewer's responses were in the form of open questions, respectful listening, rolling with and reframing resistance and affirmation. The reader will note that, at some points, there might exist the temptation to confront. The interviewer, however, remained empathic and avoided arguments and/or other roadblocks that could harm the atmosphere of client-generated problem identification. Clients are often surprised and relieved at this; instead of resisting, they tend to be willing to continue the self-evaluation/disclosure process.

The client has identified "where he hurts" and the interviewer invites him to go there. This hurt is coupled with a major discrepancy in the client's life – to be a good father. This is enough motivation to begin the contemplation stage of change where the client is invited to explore the hurt (guilt). Now in the contemplation stage of change the interviewer implements aspects of treatment to assist the client in emotional regulation and distress tolerance of the "guilt." The interviewer is NOT ignoring the alcohol use (abuse/dependency) nor the depressive disorder nor the obvious interaction between the two. They are both in the pre-contemplation stage of change and will be treated accordingly when the client is in a "stage of readiness" to work on those issues.

The Contemplation Stage Of Change

Interviewer: I'm glad to see you…how has your week been?

Client: Miserable…my wife just won't leave it alone about the drinking and the DUI's, I think her sister is encouraging her to divorce me…and my son is at the point where he walks out of the room when I walk in.

Interviewer: It sounds very stressful…and very frightening.

Client: That's a good word…frightening. I can't take all of this… DUI's, no job, money problems, wife problems, kid problems.

Interviewer: How are you managing all of this?

Client: I hide…seriously. I stay in bed most of the day…I don't sleep, I just stay in bed. And then at night I go to the bar and hang out with my buddies. I'll tell you…thank heavens for them, going to the bar at night is the only thing keeping me sane.

Interviewer: How is that working for you and how are the suicidal thoughts?

Client: You mean staying in bed and going to the bar?

Interviewer: Yes…as coping strategies, how are they working for you?

Client: Well, for one thing, my buddies make me feel better…feel better about myself…and the alcohol…well…the alcohol makes the pain numb.

Interviewer: The "pain"—the "guilt"—we touched on previously? The alcohol numbs the guilt?

Client: OK…you could say that.

Interviewer: Based on what we talked about…that is what I'm hearing…can we talk more about you and this feeling of guilt?

Client: Well, I'm good at it…feeling guilt and shame…I learned from the master, my old man…he never let go of a chance to find something wrong with me.

Interviewer: I can understand you feeling all types of emotions when we look at your early experiences…anger, shame, guilt…they are all very understandable. And also, what is understandable, is your need to manage these emotions and you found alcohol very useful.

Client: OK…since you put it that way…I see where you're going.

Interviewer: It's a confusing situation isn't it? That which has helped you manage pain for most of your life can also create havoc in your life…like the DUI.

Client: I don't know…you take the good with the bad, I guess.

Interviewer: Are you open to talking about other ways to manage this guilt?

Client: And quit drinking? There is more to my drinking than just making me feel better…I like the taste…and I bond through Budweiser.

Interviewer: Giving you options...so that if, or when, you decide that alcohol is not in your best interest...you have other ways to manage the pain that life brings and, maybe, different ways to form relationships.

Client: So, you're not telling me I have to quit drinking tomorrow...I think. You're trying to tell me that I drink for a number of reasons.

Interviewer: Correct.

Client: I've felt like this my whole life...that I fail at everything...I'm worthless. How can I get rid of that?

Interviewer: Not "get rid of;" that's what alcohol does...for a short time. We're talking management, not elimination, and we'll talk about it...and we'll keep talking until we find what works to help you.

Client: I hope it works...

Interviewer: Well...what we've done today is focus on this guilt/shame issue which could be one of the factors that makes alcohol so helpful and attractive to you. We've agreed to look at other ways to manage these very common, understandable and painful feelings, and we are going to talk about some things and see if they work for you...and, if they don't we'll keep talking until we find what works.

Commentary: The therapy moved to the contemplation stage of change due to a major motivating discrepancy being discovered rather quickly and the interviewer deciding to act on it. Remember, going to where the client hurts is the first order of business. The interviewer, using some select skills, moved quickly out of contemplation and generated the client's desire to move toward preparation stage of change for skills enhancement in emotional regulation, distress tolerance, and relationship effectiveness.

The Preparation
Stage Of Change

Interviewer: Good to see you...how was this past week?

Client: Well...both good and bad.

Interviewer: A lot like life.

Client: I guess...I've tried some of the skills we talked about but the tavern called out my name last night.

Interviewer: Well...let's talk about it.

Client: My wife and I had a huge fight over one of her credit card bills. And then my son called me the same name I used to call my old man when he was drunk...that was way too much...I tried the opposite to action thing we talked about...I tried to repair the situation by apologizing to my wife for my anger, and I did feel better but, then, she attacked me for being a phony and I just left the house and went to the bar.

Interviewer: That must have been disappointing...what did you learn?

Client: Well...I'm paying much more attention to myself...I trigger into rage when I'm not in control of things...and when my wife spent that money without checking with me first I went nuts. And then my son's name-calling...

Interviewer: Sounds like you handled it well....what did you enter in your journal last night?

Client: Well...alcohol is my best friend...it has great advantages for me. It helps me gain friends, helps me feel better about myself, helps me forget painful stuff...and I like the taste. But, I think, I'm paying a price for this...my son. I love that kid beyond words. Do you want to hear a story? You know when I promised myself that I would be a better father than my old man...he had just beaten me senseless...I was 13...he broke my jaw, wrist...and two ribs. Before I got to the hospital, lying on my bed...I made that promise.

Interviewer: This isn't the way you wanted to be, is it? I have a sense that you are at your best...and happiest...when you and your son are doing well together...I think...in a way...raising your son is your "passion."

Client: I think that's true...my happiest moments are when I am with him...when I see him happy...I fear I've lost him...that's the shame...I've screwed up the most fun and important job I'll ever have.

Interviewer: I think it might be helpful to look at some things that might help repair this relationship. We are certainly going to continue looking at your shame and how it controls some of your behaviors...but...I sense...you want to talk also about this relationship...so let's do that.

Commentary: The door is open for the client to enter the preparation and action stages of change with the therapist using aspects of treatment to help repair this relationship. Work now will focus on behavioral strategies by which the client may operate in a constructive fashion with his son. Continued insight may be provided the client on the influence of "shame" in his actions and how to manage this emotion with reminders of his skill sets. From the aspect of "where the client is" on readiness to change, we see him in the preparation/action stage of change with his shameful emotions; the preparation stage of change for his relationship with his son; and in the pre-contemplation stage of change for alcohol dependency and depressive disorders. Now, we hope to move the client to the action stage of change with shameful emotions; action stage of change with his relationship with his son; and the contemplation stage of change for alcohol dependency and depressive disorder.

The Preparation
Stage Of Change

Interviewer: Nice to see you....how has your week been?

Client: My son walks out of the room when I walk in....what does that tell you about how my week has been?

Interviewer: You have feelings of anger...and based on what we have been talking about what other feelings are experienced when he does that?

Client: Those feelings of shame and guilt come up...and then all I want to do is get to the bar and be with my buddies and down a few beers to calm down...I know all that. But...and I hope you believe this...I have not been going to the bar that often...I've been using that "self-soothing" stuff we've been talking about... and it seems to help.

Interviewer: You are using some other ways to manage your guilt...other than alcohol. Remember...feelings just "are"...they don't define us...the alcohol is used to eliminate...briefly...those uncomfortable emotions. The skills you are practicing will help in managing those emotions.

Client: I guess...but what do I do about him...I'm taking care of me...but what about my relationship with him. You know, not long ago we used to have a routine of having breakfast together. But while he was eating cereal I was having my "jump-start" breakfast... two fingers of Jim Beam and two Buds...that was my breakfast. I quit doing that because he was complaining to his mother about it...and because I would do anything to make him happy.

Interviewer: How long ago did that happen...when you quit your "jump-start" breakfast?

Client: About nine months before I was fired.

Interviewer: I see...and now what has been happening?

Client: He doesn't eat with me at all...he totally avoids me...just like I avoided my old man...he pretends I don't exist. I just want him back...I want him to be my buddy again.

Interviewer: This avoiding you...that appears to be the major problem in the relationship...you just want a chance to do things with him again.

Client: That's it...right there.

Interviewer: Let's talk about a few things to make that happen... what changes would you like to see?

Client: I don't know...we used to do all kind of things together... we were joined at the hip...I want to go back to that.

Interviewer: What can we discuss to make that happen?

Client: Well, we both love baseball...and we have that minor league team in Kalamazoo...we could go to a game. . . .

Interviewer: That's a good starting point...you are a good father...you can get back there. Let's talk about any issues that could make that plan work or not work.

Client: Well, my energy level for one thing. And...I'd have to give up a night or two with my buddies at the bar.

Interviewer: Sounds like there would have to be some changes you would make. Would you like to discuss these issues...because we would like this plan to be a success.

Client: No...I'm optimistic...I want my son back...we'll go to a game tonight.

Interviewer: OK...things are stressful at home...the real stressor is your relationship with your son. Your wish is to go back to the time when you and your son were very close...you miss that. Your thought is to take him to a ball game and see if that can start a better relationship?

Client: I hope it works...I think it will. My father never did anything with us. What do I do if he says "no"?

Interviewer: Then we work together and either adjust the plan or go to a new one. Remember, being a good father is important for you.

Commentary: We now move into the action stage of change on the client's issue of his relationship with his son. We will implement the cognitive behavioral therapy skills designed for that stage of change and begin to move the client to the contemplation stage of change for his alcohol dependency and depressive disorder.

The Action Stage Of Change

Interviewer: Good to see you...how was this past week and how did the plan go?

Client: Well...both good and bad.

Interviewer: A lot like life.

Client: I guess...we went to a ballgame on Tuesday night. It was a great game. We went to dinner first and talked baseball and stuff...it felt so good.

Interviewer: So, he didn't say "no."

Client: Right...he was excited. It was going well until the fifth inning of the game. I was getting thirsty. I went to the concession stand and got him a pop and I bought a beer. When I got back to the seats he saw the beer, and he didn't say a word to me the rest of the night. It was only one beer...I wasn't drunk. My drinking affects him, doesn't it? It ruined the whole night...I felt miserable...guilty...in your words. I knew it all along...I just didn't want to deal with it.

Interviewer: So...what happened after the game?

Client: I desperately needed a drink and to go to the bar to be with my buddies. But, I used some of those skills you've been talking to me about...I tried the self-soothing stuff, but the big issue was that opposite action stuff and I went to apologize to him. My drinking hurts him...just like it hurt me as a kid...I thought my alcohol didn't hurt my son, because I've never hit him...but it does hurt him. I've got to quit drinking...I've got to... but it scares me. We are going to another game tonight and I promised him there would be no alcohol. I've been trying to cut back this week...I want my son back.

Interviewer: You want to be a good father...you want to change behaviors because of that. How have the attempts at cutting back been for you?

Client: Not well...I get really depressed and nervous when I go too long, and I'm going to miss my friends at the bar and that energized feeling...

Interviewer: This will be a struggle, but we'll work through this...because you are motivated...you want to be a good father.

Commentary: The client has reached the contemplation stage of change for alcohol dependency and depressive disorders. His suicide risk was moderated by giving him management of his locus of pain.

He was placed in a dually-diagnosed enhanced detox program which treated the depression with appropriate medical interventions. He remains in the action stage of change for his shame/guilt and in the action stage of change for his relationship with his son. His therapy lasted nine months. As of the writing of this book, he has been sober for 19 years. His son received his Master's degree in social work and now works as an addiction counselor. This case study appears in this book with their permission.

Case Study for Readers

As we conclude our conversation on treatment principles, I would offer the reader an exercise. The following is a case conceptualization of a young man with multiple stressors. Formulate a treatment plan for him based upon the issues discussed in this book. Issues to be considered would be: 1) Assess risk for suicide and give reasons; 2) In what areas would he be seen as being in the pre-contemplation stage of change; 3) Identify the locus of his pain and where you would start your therapy; 4) What would your treatment plan look like?

This 17-year-old high school senior appears for his interview ten minutes late due to "being stuck in traffic." His mother, who transported him, did not accompany him to the office. He is a tall, thin young man who is appropriately and casually dressed. His posture and gait are unremarkable and there were no distinguishing physical characteristics. He immediately slumps in his chair and makes an obvious effort to avoid eye contact. He was referred here at the order of the Drug Court for a charge of DUI with the result of a suspended license until his twenty-first birthday. He appears lethargic with an economy of responses and a quiet, distant voice volume. Mood and affect are flat and it is difficult to gauge if this presentation is designed to passively convey his anger over the court order or if it is diagnostic of a mood or anxiety disorder. He appears oriented to time, place, person, and reason for interview. Memory, both recent and remote, is intact. He does not display any distorted, delusional, or bizarre thinking. Insight is limited. Defensiveness is remarkable with rationalizing and resignation being predominant. Reliability of some factual material in this interview is guarded.

When invited by this interviewer to talk about himself, he hesitated as if unfamiliar with such a request. He finally asks the interviewer for structure with a "what do you want to know?" question. When further encouraged to openly discuss himself with an open-ended questions he begins to focus on his recent legal trouble. He is quite defensive at this point and goes to great lengths to point out that he is "not an alcoholic." When encouraged to focus on that issue he explains the situation of being stopped by the police after "having two beers" at a friend's house. He goes on to blame the police for "picking on" him due to his "reputation" in his small community. When asked to expand on his "reputation" he explains that he had been in trouble before; starting at the age of 11 for destruction of property. He was put on probation for two years and defined that experience as "a joke." He becomes somewhat animated when discussing his various other run-ins with legal authorities and appears to enjoy the excitement of getting in and out of trouble. He could be described as bragging about his legal troubles.

He holds a dim view of school and "can't wait" to be finished. He has no plans for the future other than "I might join the Army." It appears from his report that he has significant academic and social challenges in the school setting. He cannot remember a time when school was enjoyable or rewarding. He is not involved in any social, academic, or athletic activities in the school setting.

When questioned about family he becomes quite hesitant and responds, "not much to say." In response to direct questions, he reveals that he doesn't know his biological father and his mother has had numerous boyfriends throughout the years. Some of these men, he describes as "nice" but "didn't stick around very long." Others he describes in very derogatory terms. He denies any history of physical or sexual abuse, but reliability here is questioned. He describes his mother as "depressed" and he fears that she is "an alcoholic." He has no siblings; but had a younger brother who died of unknown causes when the client was six. Mother works two jobs and periodically gets financial help from an "uncle" of his. He questions the exact relationship of this man to the mother, but does not pursue this subject further. The current relationship between mother and the client is under much stress due, in large part, to the DUI. She was hoping for him to acquire employment after school ended, but the legal charge "makes that a problem" due to transportation issues. He deals with this subject rather casually, demonstrating perhaps, a lack of empathy or significant anger toward the mother.

When encouraged to discuss history of substance use he becomes defensive and points out this interviewer's connection to the court and legal system. The interviewer validates that concern and gives a description of the office's services and its relationship to the court. The explanation has no impact on the client and does diminish his defensiveness. He explains that he started drinking at seven years of age, likes the taste of alcohol, will never experiment with any other drug, and sees real social and behavioral advantages to alcohol use. All of his friends are "drinkers" and "we all get rowdy together." He likes the way alcohol makes him feel and adds "people like me better when I'm drunk." He has no plans to give up drinking and is quite animated at declaring his "right to drink." When asked about his first experience with alcohol at the age of seven he would only say that he "was having problems with my mother" and the alcohol "got me away from thinking about it."

When asked about his friends, he responds with another "not much to say" comment. He describes them all as being "pretty much" like him. When asked further questions about his friends he withdraws and becomes quite passive. He then states, "when I die they'll be able to have my funeral in a phone booth." The interviewer reflects an empathic response focused on loneliness and the client looks away. He then asks when the interview would be over. The interviewer responds with an affirmation, an empathic reflection of his discomfort, and asks him for a history of suicidality.

He responds with, "nobody would miss me if I died" and, "my mom would be better off." He indicates that he "thinks about it a lot" but "only when I'm sober" and adds that being drunk allows him to "turn it off." He denies any history of attempts and/or gestures. He denies current intent. He agrees to a verbal agreement to call our service to contact me at any time when suicide thoughts become intrusive. He states that, "when I'm alone" would be a crisis time.

As the session is concluding, the interviewer questions him about scars on his arm reflective of burns and cuts. He responds openly to the question and indicates that he has been "burning" and "cutting" since age 14 and, more often than not, cuts with his girlfriend. He claims it "chills me" and "gets me high." He adds: "I'm kind of addicted to it now." He shows no hesitancy or embarrassment in discussing this matter and, in fact, appears quite animated while engaged on the topic. He claims to "burn only when I'm angry" and describes his anger as quite aggressive. When asked if the cutting has a similar effect on him as alcohol, he responds, "kind of...but it makes me feel mellow."

The session concludes with the interviewer summarizing the session and reflecting that "loneliness" appears to be an issue in the client's life. He quietly agrees: "It's been that way my whole life." When offered an opportunity to "look at this" next session, he responds with, "I thought this was about my drinking." The interviewer responds that this is "his" time and we will talk about what he wants to talk about. He responds with, "I'll think about it."

Conclusion

In 1992, the American Association of Suicidology dedicated a mission statement with the goal of reducing the suicide rate in the United States to single digits by the end of that decade. The U.S. rate of suicide at that time was 10.9 per 100,000 of our population. That noble mission statement failed. In fact, the rate of suicide in our country has remained steady at 10 to 13 per 100,000 for over 80 years. The only remarkable decline in that rate was during the years of World War II when the rate from 1942 to 1946 declined to the 8 to 9 per 100,000 range. This fascinating and disturbing feature is due to many factors. The most important factor, in my estimation, is the tragic misdirection of what is often termed "suicide prevention" programs.

We have programs today that do marvelous work in training and educating our citizens about suicide. These programs teach about the dynamics of suicide, the risk factors to suicide, and the warning signs to a pending suicide crisis. We have a long overdue respect for the unbearable grief of men, women and children who lose a loved one to suicide. We have crisis intervention programs that allow us to capture the at-risk person and guide them to help. We have pharmacological interventions that decrease the pain of mood, anxiety, and psychotic disorders. And yet, the suicide rates remain unmoved. Are these efforts useless? Of course not. They are, merely, not enough. We need a change of direction.

I do fear that we have today, and have had for decades, an overemphasis on mental illnesses. We have, unfortunately, "medicalized" and "biologized" suicide. We often hear that "depression causes suicide." That is a tragically misleading comment. There is no one isolated "causal" entity in regards to suicide. There is no "golden key" to explain this tragedy. Certainly, as we have pointed out in this book, depression is a major correlate and risk factor to suicide. That means that when a suicide does occur there is a 70% chance that the victim of that act was experiencing the symptoms of this disorder. Depression, however, in its varied forms is experienced by millions of our citizens in any given year. Only a fraction of men and women with depression go on to die by suicide. Is it not interesting that the use of highly effective anti-depressant medications has not reduced the rate of suicide? We also know that suicide is the result of a complexity of issues. It is the sad result of varied stressors, causing individually defined agony, for which the person has no capacity to cope.

Today's "suicide prevention" efforts are, more often than not, focused on the early detection and treatment of mood and anxiety disorders. Is this a worthwhile endeavor? It certainly is. Will this decrease the rate of suicide in our society? It helps...but it is not the total answer. Can we prevent an individual's suicide? We can if we get the chance. Can we reduce the overall number of suicides? I believe this is possible with a sincere change in the focus of prevention. Can we ever eradicate and completely eliminate the suicide tragedy in our society? I do not believe this is possible. But, in order to achieve this possible reduction in rates, we need a serious change in our approach to prevention.

The goal of suicide is the elimination of pain. This pain may be due to a mental illness, a tragic loss, a personal failure, a destitute life, loneliness. In many ways, our prevention efforts are also oriented towards "elimination of pain." However, we need a more realistic focus on "coping" with pain as opposed to "eliminating" pain. Teaching our children how to cope would be an excellent starting point to suicide prevention. Suicide, in its essence, is a result of a failure in the individual's capacity to cope.

What else can we teach our children that may act as protective factors in their lives when that inevitable pain hits them? It starts with allowing them to feel pain, failure, disappointment, sadness, frustration, and all the other discomforting emotions that life brings to our table. All too often we either "protect" our kids from feeling discomfort or diminish the impact of an upsetting event. By remaining empathic to the child's pain, we impress upon them the attitude that "it is understandable you feel this way." Instead, we often position ourselves in a way that uncomfortable emotions are cast as an exception and not an expectation.

We teach them to pay attention to life. We also teach them to pay attention to their world. When I was a child, it was a tradition in my home to take a car ride every Sunday afternoon. The goal of the car ride, according to my father, was to "get lost" and figure a way to get home. I didn't get it as a kid, but now I do...thankfully. He called these Sunday excursions "taking the scenic route." It was an essential on these rides to pay attention since there was a "debriefing" that night as to what we saw on the ride and how we ever "got back home." My father was fond of car rides and always took the "scenic route." On his death bed, his last words: "Jack, don't forget to take the scenic route."

We teach our children resiliency. We teach them to bounce back from adversity. We make our children feel loved and accepted unconditionally. We teach them that there is nothing that could happen that could make us stop loving them. We teach our children boundaries to their behaviors and skills to regulate their emotions. We teach them social skills and communication

skills and the joy of having friends. And we teach them hope...
hope for the future and the self-awareness and self-efficacy to
appreciate the future as their "chance."

Finally, thank you for reading this book and feel free to contact
me with questions, concerns, issues at jackklott@aol.com.

References

Chapter One

American Psychiatric Association. (1994). *Diagnostic and statistical manual of mental disorders* (4th ed.).Washington, DC: American Psychiatric Association.

Barraclough, B.M., Bunch, J., & Sainsbury, T. (1974). One hundred cases of suicide: Clinical aspects. *British Journal of Psychiatry, 125,* 355-373.

Bowlby, J. (1988). *A secure base: Parent-child attachment and healthy human development.* New York: Basic Books.

Chapman, P.L. & Mullis, R.L. (2000). Racial differences in adolescent coping and self-esteem. *Journal of Genetic Psychology, 161,* 151-160.

Clark, D.C. & Fawcett, J.A. (1992). Review of empirical risk factors for evaluation of the suicidal patient. New York: Oxford University Press.

Clark, D.C. (1992). Assessment in absentia: The value of the psychological autopsy method for studying antecedents of suicide and predicting future suicides. In: R.W. Maris, A.L. Berman, J.T. Maltsberger, & R.I. Yufit (Eds.). Assessment and prediction of suicide (pp. 144-182). New York: Guilford Press.

Cornelius, J.R., Salloum, I.M., & Mezzich, J. (1995). Disproportionate suicidality in patients with comorbid major depression and alcoholism. *American Journal of Psychiatry, 152,* 358-364.

Dunner, D.L., Gershon, E.S., & Goodwin, F.K. (1976). Heritable factors in the severity of affective illness. *Biology of Psychology, 11,* 31-42.

Foa, E.B., Keane, T.M., Friedman, M.J., & Cohen, J.A. (2009). *Effective treatments for PTSD* (2nd ed.) New York: The Guilford Press.

Fonagy, P. (1997, October). *Conference for attachment and the borderline personality disorder.* Belmont, MA: Stanton Lecture.

Gold, S.N. (2000). *Not trauma alone.* New York: Routledge.

Goldston, D.B. (2008). Cultural considerations in adolescent suicide. *American Psychologist, 65,* 14-27

Goodwin, F.K. & Jamison, K.R. (1990). *Manic-depressive illness.* New York: Oxford University Press.

Gunderson, J.G. (1985). The interface between borderline personality and affective disorders. *American Journal of Psychiatry, 142,* 277-288.

Herman, J. (1992). *Trauma and recovery.* New York: Basic Books.

Jacobs, D.G. & Brown, H.N. (Eds.). (1989). Suicide: Understanding and responding. *Harvard Medical School Perspective.* Madison, CT: International University Press.

Klerman, G.L. (1987). Clinical epidemiology of suicide. *Journal of Clinical Psychology, 48,* 33-38.

Linehan, M.M. (1993). *Cognitive-behavioral treatment of borderline personality disorder.* New York: The Guilford Press.

Linehan, M.M., Armstrong, H.E., Suarez, A., Allman,D., & Heard, H.L. (1999). Cognitive behavioral treatment of chronically parasuicidal borderline clients. *Archives of General Psychiatry, 48,* 1060-1064.

Maris, R.W., Berman, A.L., Maltsberger, J.T., & Yufit, R.I. (1992). *Assessment and prediction of suicide.* New York: The Guilford Press.

Miller, A.L., Rathus, J.H., & Linehan, M.M. (2007). *Dialectical behavior therapy with suicidal adolescents.* New York: The Guilford Press.

Moscicki, E.K. (1999). Epidemiology of suicide. *International Psychogeriatric Journal, 7,* 137-148.

Muehrer, PM. 1995). Suicide and sexual orientatioin. *Journal of Suicide and Life-Threatening Behavior. 25,* 72-81.

Murphy, G.E., Davidson, R., & Slattery, J. (2003). *British Journal of Psychiatry, 252,* 347.

Noreik, K. (1984). Attempted suicide in functional psychosis. *Acta Psychiatriac Scandinavia, 52,* 81-106.

Patsiokas, A. (1979). Cognitive characteristics in suicide attempters. *Journal of Consulting and Clinical Psychology, 47,* 478-484.

Rihmer, Z., Barsi, J., Arata, M, Demeter, E. (1990). Suicide in subtypes of primary major depression. *Journal of Affective Disorders, 18,*221-225.

Rich, C.L., Young, J.G., & Fowler, R.C. (1986). San Diego Suicide Study: Young vs. Old Subjects. *Archives of General Psychiatry, 43,* 577-582.

Robins, E., Murphy, G.E., & Wilkinson, R.H. (1959). Some clinical considerations in the prevention of suicide based on a study of 134 completed suicides. *American Journal of Psychiatry, 115,*724-733.

Roy, A., (1995). Suicide among psychiatric inpatients. *Suicide and Life Threatening Behaviors, 25,* 199-202.

Sansone, R.A. (2004). Chronic suicidality and the borderline personality. *Journal of Personality Disorders, 18,* 215-225.

Schweizer, E., Dever, A., & Clary, C. (1988). Suicide upon recovery from depression. *Journal of Nervous and Mental Disorders, 176,*633-636.

Shea, S.C. (1999). *The practical art of suicide assessment.* New York: John Wiley.

Shneidman, E.S. (1985). *Definition of suicide.* New York: John Wiley.

Sullivan, H.S. (1954). *The psychiatric interview.* New York: W.W. Norton.

Stallone, F., Dunner, D.L., Ahearn, J., & Fieve, R.R. (1990). Statistical prediction of suicide in depressives. *Comprehensive Psychiatry, 21,* 381-387.

Stengel, E. (1964). *Suicide and attempted suicide.* New York: Penguin Press.

Virkkunen, M. (1996). Suicides in schizophrenia and paranoid psychosis. *British Journal of Psychiatry, 128,* 47-49.

Weeke, A., & Vaeth, M. (1999). Examination of mortality in bipolar patients. *Journal of Affective Disorders, 11,* 227-234.

Williams, J.M.G., Dalby, D., Kunar, W., & Prasad, A. (2008). Autobiographical memory and emotional disorders. In T. Dalgleish & C. Brewin. *Autobiographical Memory and Emotional Disorder: A Special Issue of Memory.* New Jersey: Psychology Press.

Reich, T., Clayton, P.J., & Winokur, G. (1969). Family history studies: V. the genetics of mania. *American Journal of Psychiatry, 125,* 1358-1369.

Yip, K.S. (2005). A multidimensional perspective of adolescent self-mutilation. *Child and Adolescent Mental Health, 10,* 80-86.

Chapter Two

Berman, A.L., Maltsberger, J.T., Maris, R.W., & Yufit, R.I. (1994). *Assessment and prediction of suicide.* New York: The Guilford Press.

Bernstein, E.M. & Putnam, F.W. (1986). Development, reliability, and validity of a dissociation scale. *Journal of Mental Disorders, 174,* 727-734.

Clark, D.C. (1992). Assessment in absentia: The value of the psychological autopsy method for studying antecedents of suicide and predicting future suicides. In: R.W. Maris, A.L. Berman, J.T. Maltsberger, & R.I. Yufit (Eds.). *Assessment and prediction of suicide* (pp. 144-182). New York: Guilford Press.

Farberow, N.L. (1980). *The many faces of suicide: indirect self-destructive behavior.* New York: McGraw-Hill.

Favazza, A. (1989). Why patients mutilate themselves. *Hospital Community Psychiatry, 40,* 137-145.

Favazza, A.R., & Rosenthal, R.J. (1993). Diagnostic issues in self-mutilation. *Hospital Community Psychiatry, 44,* 134-140.

Favazza, A. (1996). *Bodies under siege: Self-mutilation and body modification in culture and psychiatry.* Baltimore: John Hopkins University Press.

Fonagy, P. (1997, October). *Conference for attachment and the borderline personality disorder.* Belmont, MA: Stanton Lecture.

Goodstein, J. (1982). Cognitive characteristics in suicide attempters. *Archives of General Psychiatry, 43,* 674-684.

Herman, J.L., Perry, J.C., & van der Kolk, B.A. (1989). Childhood trauma in borderline personality disorders. *American Journal of Psychiatry, 146,* 490-495.

Jacobs, D.G. (1999). *Suicide assessment and intervention.* San Francisco: Jossey-Bass Publishers.

Levenson, M. (1973). Cognitive and perceptual factors in suicidal individuals. *Journal of Consulting and Clinical Psychology, 37,* 433-436.

Linehan, M.M. (1993). *Cognitive-behavioral treatment of borderline personality disorder.* New York: The Guilford Press.

Linehan, M.M., Miller, A.L., & Rathus, J.H (2007). *Dialectical behavior therapy with suicidal adolescents.* New York: The Guilford Press.

Maris, R.W., Berman, A.L., Maltsberger, J.T., & Yufit, R.I. (1992). *Assessment and prediction of suicide.* New York: The Guilford Press.

Menninger, K.A. (1938). *Man against himself.* Orlando, FL: Harcourt.

Pattison, E.M. & Kahan, J. (1983). The deliberate self-harm syndrome. *American Journal of Psychiatry, 140,* 867-872.

Roy, A. & Linniola, A. (1990). Attempted suicide in chronic schizophrenia. *British Journal of Psychiatry, 154,* 303-306.

Rudd, M.D. (2001). *Treating suicidal behavior.* New York: Guilford Press.

Sabbath, J.C. (1969). The suicidal adolescent: The expendable child. *Journal of the American Academy of Child Psychiatry, 8,* 272-289.

Saunders, B. & Giolas, M.H. (1991). Dissociation and childhood trauma in psychologically disturbed adolescents. *American Journal of Psychiatry, 148,* 50-54.

Selekman, H. (2004). *The self-harming adolescent.* New York: Guilford Press.

Shneidman, E.S. (1993). Commentary: Suicide as psychache. *Journal of Mental Disorders, 181,* 147-149.

Shneidman, E.S. (1996). *The suicidal mind.* New York: Oxford University Press.

Stack, S. (1997). Homicide followed by suicide: An analysis of Chicago data. *Criminology, 35,* 435-453.

Sullivan, H.S. (1954). *The psychiatric interview.* New York: W.W. Norton

Winchell, R.M. & Stanley, M. (1991). Self-injurious behavior: A review of the behavior and biology of self-mutilation. *American Journal of Psychiatry, 148,* 306-317.

Chapter Three

Alexopoulos, G.S. (2007). The primary care setting: A key to suicide prevention. *Advancing Suicide Prevention, Sp.Ed.,* 24-25.

Beck, A.T., Brown, G., Berchick, R.J., Steart, B.L., & Steer, R.A. (1990). Relationship between hopelessness and ultimate suicide: A replication with psychiatric outpatients. *American Journal of Psychiatry, 147,* 190-195.

Beck, A.T., Resnick, H.L.P., & Lettieri, D.J. (1974) *The prediction of suicide.* Bowie, MD: Charles Press.

Buglas, D. & Horton, J. (1974). A scale for predicting subsequent suicide behavior. *British Journal of Psychiatry, 124,* 573-578.

Clark, D. C., Young, M. A., Scheftner, W.A., Fawcett, J., & Fogg, L. (1987). A field test of Motto's risk estimator for suicide. *American Journal of Psychiatry, 144,* 923-926.

Cohen, E., Motto, J.A., & Seiden, R.H. (1986). An instrument for evaluating suicide potential: A preliminary study. *American Journal of Psychiatry, 122,* 886-891.

Cohen, J. (1989). Statistical approaches to suicide risk factor analysis. *Annals of the New York Academy of Sciences, 487,* 34-41.

Cull, J.G. & Gill, W.S. (1982). *Suicide Probability Scale.* Los Angeles: Western Psychological Services.

Dean, R.A., Miskimins, W., DeCook, R., Wilson, L.T., & Maley, R.F. (1997). Prediction of suicide in a psychiatric hospital. *Journal of Clinical Psychology, 23,* 296-301.

Eyman, S.K. & Eyman, J.R. (1992). Suicide risk and assessment instruments. *Issues, Assessments, and Interventions, 18,* 49-57.

Farberow, N.L., & MacKinnon, D.R. (1975). Prediction of suicide: A replication study. *Journal of Personality Assessment, 39,* 497-501.

Graham, J.R. (2006). MMPI-2 (4th Ed.). *Assessing personality and psychopathology.* New York: Oxford University Press.

Jacobs, D.G. (1999). *Suicide assessment and intervention.* San Francisco: Jossey-Bass Publishers.

Lettieri, D.J. (1974). Research issues in developing prediction scales. In C. Neuringer (Ed.). *Psychological assessment of suicidal risk* (pp.43-73). Springfield, IL: Charles C. Thomas.

Linehan, M.M., Goodstein, J.L., Nielson, S.L., & Chiles, J.K. (1983). Reasons for staying alive when you are thinking of killing yourself: The reasons for living inventory. *Journal of Consulting and Clinical Psychology, 51,* 276-286.

Maris, R.W., Berman, A.L., Maltsberger, J.T., & Yufit, R.I. (1992). *Assessment and prediction of suicide.* New York: The Guilford Press.

Motto, J.A., Heilbron, D.C., & Juster, R.P. (1985). Development of a clinical instrument to estimate suicide risk. *American Journal of Psychiatry, 142,* 680-686.

Pallis, D.J., Gibbons, J.S., & Pierce, D.W. (1984). Estimating suicide risk among attempted suicides: Efficiency of predictive scales after the attempt. *British Journal of Psychiatry, 144,* 139-148.

Patterson, W.M., Dohn, H.H., Bird, J., & Patterson, G.A. (1983). Evaluation of suicide patients: The SAD PERSONS scale. *Psychosomatics, 24,* 343-352.

Pierce, D.W. (1981). The predictive validity of a suicide intent scale: A five-year follow up. *British Journal of Psychiatry, 139,* 391-396.

Plutchik, R., van Praag, H.M., Conte, H.R., & Picard, S. (1999). Correlates of suicide and violence risk: The Suicide Risk Measure. *Comprehensive Psychiatry, 30,* 296-302.

Reynolds, W.M. (1997). *The Suicide Ideation Questionnaire.* Odessa, FL: Psychological Assessment Resources.

Roberts, M. (1997). *The Man Who Listens to Horses.* New York: Random House.

Sullivan, H.S. (1954). *The Psychiatric Interview.* New York: W.W. Norton

Tuckman, J. & Youngman, W.F. (1988). Assessment of suicide risk in attempted suicides. In H.L.P. Resnick (Ed.). *Suicide Behaviors: Diagnosis and Management* (pp. 190-197). Boston, MA: Little and Brown.

Zung, W.W.K. (1996). Index of Potential Suicide (IPS): A rating scale for suicide prevention. *The Prediction of Suicide,* 221-249.

Chapter Four

American Psychiatric Association. (2000). *Diagnostic and statistical manual of mental disorders* (4th ed., text revision).Washington, DC: American Psychiatric Association.

Berman, P.S. (1997). *Case Conceptualization and Treatment Planning.* Thousand Oaks, CA: Sage Publications.

Dean, P.J., & Range, L.M. (1996). The escape theory of suicide and perfectionism. *Death Studies, 20,* 415-424.

Fawcett, J.A. (1988). Predictors of early suicide identification and appropriate intervention. *Journal of Clinical Psychiatry, 49,* 7-8.

Fawcett, J.A. (1995). Assessing and treating the patient at risk for suicide. *Psychiatric Annals, 23,* 244-255.

Hellman, I.D., Morrison, T.L., & Abramowitz, S.I. (1986). The stresses of psychotherapeutic work: A replication and extension. *Journal of Clinical Psychiatry, 42,* 197-205.

Klott, J.O. & Jongsma, A.E. (2004). *The suicide and homicide risk assessment and prevention treatment planner.* Hoboken, NJ: John Wiley & Sons.

Lewis, L.M. (2007). No-harm contracts: A review of what we know. *Suicide and Life-Threatening Behavior, 37 (1),* 50-57.

Linehan, M.M. (1993). *Cognitive-behavioral treatment of borderline personality disorder.* New York: Guilford Press.

Linehan, M.M., Armstrong, H.E., & Suarez, A. (1999). Cognitive-behavioral treatment of chronically parasuicidal borderline patients. *Archives of General Psychiatry, 48,* 1060-1064.

Maris, S. (1981). *Pathways to suicide: A survey of self-destructive behaviors.* Baltimore, MD: John Hopkins University Press.

Meichenbaum, D. (2009). *Core tasks.* New York: Rutledge Publishing.

Miller, A.L., Rathus, J.H., & Linehan, M.M. (2007). *Dialectical behavior therapy with suicidal adolescents.* New York: The Guilford Press.

Miller, W. & Rollnick, S. (2002). *Motivational interviewing: Helping people change.* Hoboken, NJ: Wiley & Sons.

Prochaska, J.O., Norcross, J.C., & DiClemente, C.C. (1994). *Changing for good: The revolutionary program that explains six stages of change and teaches you to free yourself from bad habits. The transtheoretical model of change.* New York: W. Morrow.

Roswell, V.A. (1988). Professional liability: Issues for behavior therapists. *Behavior Therapist, 11,* 163-171.

Rudd, M.D. (2001). *Treating suicidal behavior.* New York: Guilford Press.

Shneidman, E.S. (1985). *Definition of suicide.* New York: Wiley & Sons.

Shneidman, E.S. (1996). *The suicidal mind.* New York: Oxford University Press.

Suicide - A problem to be solved

BR- Accurate diags = answer about why she has these struggles - Can you see a dx as a descriptive set of symptoms that help others better understand what you are exp & not a label that becomes part of who you are?

BR- Problem solving skills, emotional regulation, reduce impulsivity mgmt of anx & dep symptoms building of support network all to reduce freq & intensity of feelings not eliminate

BR- Suicide viewed, as at this time in your life, as the best solution to unremitting & intolerable pain feeling hopeless & helpless.

BR- Is self Harm behavior

unfulfilled need — (operant) - designed to achieve consequences & function to control one environment, designed to get others attention, elicit care, be taken seriously

Relief from pain — (respondent) - automatically elicited by a situation or a specific stimulous. Escape from pain - seeking of a solution.

Self Mutilation - Anti-Suicide; It keeps people from dying.

eating BR- Emotion regulation - release of tension
sleeping BR- Used to regulate difficult emotions of loneliness etc (what else - Ask her).

& others

BR- S. Ideation - various levels of stress becomes intense that death is entertained as coping strategy. Goal to remove cl. blinders & help them find other ways to resolve unbearable pain.

..lize SI & explain under right circumstances anyone to that place. SI deators very open to